D1454425

© Youth for Christ, Urban Saints and Scripture Union 2011

First published 2011

ISBN 978 1 84427 587 8

Scripture Union

207–209 Queensway, Bletchley, Milton Keynes, MK2 2EB

Email: info@scriptureunion.org.uk

Website: www.scriptureunion.org.uk

Scripture Union Australia

Locked Bag 2, Central Coast Business Centre, NSW 2252

Website: www.scriptureunion.org.au

Scripture Union USA

PO Box 987, Valley Forge, PA 19482

Website: www.scriptureunion.org

Urban Saints

Kestin House, 45 Crescent Road, Luton, LU2 0AH

Website: www.urbansaints.org

Youth For Christ

Business Park East, Unit D2, Coombswood Way, Halesowen, West Midlands, B62 8BH

Website: www.yfc.co.uk

All rights reserved. No part of this publication may be reproduced, stored in a retrieval system, or transmitted in any form or by any means, electronic, mechanical, photocopying, recording or otherwise, without the prior permission of Scripture Union.

Scriptures quoted from The Youth Bible, New Century Version (Anglicised edition) © 1993, 2000, 2007 by Authentic Media.

British Library Cataloguing-in-Publication Data

A catalogue record of this book is available from the British Library.

Printed and bound in China by 1010 Printing International Ltd.

Cover and text design: www.martinlore.co.uk

Scripture Union is an international charity working with churches in more than 130 countries, providing resources to bring the good news of Jesus Christ to children, young people and families and to encourage them to develop spiritually through the Bible and prayer.

As well as our network of volunteers, staff and associates who run holidays, church-based events and school Christian groups, we produce a wide range of publications and support those who use our resources through training programmes.

Urban Saints are passionate about working with children and young people who have no church connection, as well as those linked to a church, helping them to realise their full God-given potential as they journey from childhood to adulthood. Children and young people (aged 5 to 18+) connect with the movement in a variety of ways, including weekly youth groups, special events, holidays, community projects (both UK wide and overseas) and training programmes.

Youth for Christ (YFC) is a national Christian charity that was founded by Billy Graham in 1946. Working with around 300,000 young people each month, we draw alongside teens from every background and culture in Britain. Our 150 full-time staff and countless local volunteers specialise in working with unchurched youth: communicating and demonstrating their Christian faith.

# CONTENTS

# INTRODUCTION

## WELCOME TO DECATHLON!

*Decathlon* is a ten-session programme for young people, particularly those from outside a church community. It seeks to use sport to tell young people the gospel message and can be used in a variety of contexts. In years when major sporting events are held, such as the Olympic Games, the World Cup or Commonwealth Games, a sports programme is an ideal way to reach out to those who have not yet heard the good news of Jesus.

## REACHING OUT

*Decathlon* can be run with young people from your church, and might be a good place to help them think about how they can reach out to their non-Christian friends. However, the programme was conceived mainly for young people from outside your church community, to be used in a variety of contexts:

### School setting

The material can be used for an assembly – each session (called an 'event') starts with an assembly outline. Some of the subsequent material in each event can be adapted for use in an RE or PSHE/ citizenship session.

### Holiday group setting

*Decathlon* can be run as a youth version of a holiday club. The mix of games, activities and Bible engagement means that you can reach young people from a variety of backgrounds and introduce them to the good news of Jesus. You could run *Decathlon* every day for a week, every afternoon for two weeks, or as event days throughout the summer holidays.

### Youth group

The assembly material can also be used as a 'God slot' in an open youth group. The material can also be used as a more intentional programme for youth groups, whether in a youth cell or a Sunday morning group.

## LINKING UP

If your church is running a sports-based holiday club, such as *On Your Marks!*, then you might want to link your *Decathlon* programme with the holiday club. Providing a coordinated children's and youth club would attract families looking for things for their children and young people to do during the summer. In addition, are there opportunities for your young people to serve as helpers/young leaders on the holiday club? This would be an ideal place for young people to get involved, serving and using their gifts.

On Your Marks!
£12.99, 9781844275694
(Scripture Union)

# ABOUT DECATHLON

## THE AIMS OF DECATHLON

*Decathlon* uses sports and games as a bridge into young people's lives, to tell the good news of Jesus Christ to young people from both within and outside a church community. The programme takes young people through different areas of faith that many often have questions about. By the end of the programme, young people will have encountered the gospel message, explored how that might apply to their life and been given a chance to respond in an appropriate way.

*Decathlon* aims to:

- introduce young people from outside a church community to Jesus, as well as to Christians and church.
- explain the gospel message and give space and opportunity for young people to respond.
- create a fun, engaging programme where young people feel welcomed and valued.

## THEME

*Decathlon* is all about sport and this is a great way to make use of the buzz around events, such as the Olympic Games, the Commonwealth Games or a football World Cup. The young people will get a chance to play a different sport or game each week. You could explore how to play the sport, and in each event, you'll be provided with the website of organisations that will give help and advice to play the sport. However, each event has details of how to play a quirky version of the sport, which will be easier for you to play in an assembly or group setting, than a true version of the sport. These versions of each sport will also level the playing field for the young people, so that those who are not as good at sport (or not as interested) will be able to engage fully without feeling left out or inadequate. Some of the sports chosen here are more unusual, so this will help with levelling the playing field too.

## TEACHING PROGRAMME

*Decathlon* covers many of the 'basics' of the Christian faith. For young people from outside your church community, this will be an introduction – it will probably be the first time these young people will have encountered these ideas and they may have a variety of responses to them. If young people from your church come to your group, then this might either be a revision of things they already know and believe, or a challenge to them – what do they believe and how does that affect their whole life?

Each event is tightly linked to the day's aim, so you'll be able to focus on what you want the young people to explore and take away with them. The Bible activities are the most important part of your programme and they should be well planned, prayed through and presented clearly to allow God's Word to settle and grow in young people's minds.

Alongside this is the importance of how you relate to the young people, as this reinforces the teaching (as the young people see you 'practising what you preach'). Jesus said, 'When you welcome even a child because of me, you welcome me. And when you welcome me, you welcome the one who sent me' (Luke 9:48, CEV). So as you welcome young people, you welcome Jesus; as you talk with them, listen to their stories, laugh at their jokes and cheer their successes. However ordinary these things may be, you are doing them as if to Jesus. Treat the young people with the love, respect and dignity with which you would honour him. In addition, young people from outside a church community will start to think of Jesus/God in terms of the person who tells them about Jesus/God. You need to 'be' the message, as well as giving the message.

## EVENT 1 — GOALBALL
**Who is God?**
Key passage: Luke 15:11–32 and others
Target: to understand that we don't always need to see things with physical eyes to know they're real, and that the same is true of God.

## EVENT 2 — VOLLEYBALL
**We are part of God's plan**
Key passage: Ephesians 2:1–10
Target: to see that we are not bouncing aimlessly through life – God loves us and has got a clear direction for our lives.

## EVENT 3 — ARCHERY
**Why did Jesus die?**
Key passage: Romans 5:1–11
Target: to realise that, though we don't always get things right, God wants to give us a new start.

## EVENT 4 — DRESSAGE
**Jesus brings freedom!**
Key passages: John 8:31,32;
Matthew 7:24,25
Target: to discover that life with Jesus is not about being bound by rules that restrict us, but is about being set free by him!

## EVENT 5 — SHOT PUT
**Who sets your direction?**
Key passage: Matthew 4:17–22
Target: to explore that following God means we need to choose the right path.

## EVENT 6 — MODERN PENTATHLON
**God's gifts**
Key passage: 1 Corinthians 12
Target: to discover that God has given us all different talents, and that when we work together, we achieve more.

## EVENT 7 — FOUR-PERSON RELAY
**Serving others**
Key passage: John 13:1–17
Target: to explore the idea that Jesus calls us to think about others first, rather than only thinking about ourselves and what we can achieve.

## EVENT 8 — FENCING
**What's worth fighting for?**
Key passage: Luke 4:14–30
Target: to realise that some things are really worth fighting for – God calls us to fight for the oppressed.

## EVENT 9 — MARATHON
**With God for life!**
Key passage: Hebrews 12:1–3
Target: to understand that following Jesus isn't a quick sprint, but a race for life. We need to persevere, even when life is tough!

## EVENT 10 — GYMNASTICS
**Living for God now**
Key passage: 1 Samuel 16:1–13
Target: to understand that we can follow Jesus, and make a difference in the world now – we don't have to wait!

## PROGRAMME BREAKDOWN
The material for each event breaks down like this:

**Training for you**
This section gives you, the leader, an introduction to the theme for the event. It outlines the aim (here called the 'Target') and the key passage for the session. There are some notes for you to think about personally, as you prepare the event. Take some time to read the Bible passage and think about what issues and themes it raises for you. As is said earlier, you need to 'be' the message, as well as tell it. The two sections about the different backgrounds of young people in your group are designed to help you think about the issues that will be pertinent for these two groups. As you get to know the group better, you'll be able to think more specifically about reactions to themes and Bible stories. However, use these two paragraphs as starting points.

**Assembly/Basic talk outline**
This section is designed to be suitable for use in an assembly, 'God slot' or other event where a short talk would be most appropriate. It is in this section that the game version of the sport is described. These games can be done as demonstrations from the front, or with more general interaction – how you do this will depend on the context in which you're working.

The talk part of this section has been written specifically with young people from outside your church community in mind. And so, the language used strives to be Christian-jargon-free, and it explains concepts in simple ways. As you prepare these talks, remember to rewrite them so that they suit your style of delivery and your context. In some situations, you might include stories from your own life; in some you might need to be a little less personal.

**Resources for 11 to 14s and 14 to 18s**

These sections are designed to help you plan a longer programme – maybe an evening session, or a group that runs during the day in the school holidays. An 11-year-old is very different from a 17-year-old, and the two sections have been written to be appropriate for these younger and older age groups. However, you may feel that an activity from the 'wrong' age group fits your needs – if so, choose that!

The timings given for each activity are approximate, so that you can plan enough material for your session. According to your group, they may take different lengths of time to complete! Each of these two sections are split into:

*Introductory activity*

These are designed to introduce the theme and work towards the aim of the session, which will be achieved more comprehensively in the Bible activity. They are light-hearted and fun introductions and take the form of games, discussions and challenges. One or two activities are supplied for each age group in each event.

*Bible*

These are where the young people will encounter the main part of the aim, and where you can get them (whatever their background) engaging with the Bible and hearing from God. The teaching is done in a mixture of all-together times and group work. If you have a small group, you could work in pairs, or stay together for the whole session. Try your best, too, to let the young people discover for themselves rather than explaining too much. Young people will remember and understand more if they have come to an idea themselves.

Guidelines are given on how to help young people explore the Bible passages and themes, but if God takes you elsewhere, be ready to go with it. The aim is ideally where you'd want to be, but don't be scared to take a different course if this is where the Spirit is leading you. Again, one or two activities are given for each age group in each event.

*Response*

This is where the group can start to see how what they have discovered in the Bible activities might apply to their own lives, or affect their own thinking about God. They are a mixture of reflection, prayer and active responses, depending on the aim and theme of the event. Be ready during these times to pray with any young people who might want to, or to chat with young people in more depth (being aware of all safeguarding issues). You might want to set aside a quiet area where you meet so that young people can take time out from the session and chat with someone.

*For all groups/For church groups*

Most of the activities given in these two sections are suitable for all groups, regardless of background, and are labelled as 'For all groups'. However, there are a few that are listed as 'For church groups'. These activities are designed for you to use if you have church young people in your group. They will still explore the event's theme, but push the young people to think more deeply about the issues that arise. If you have a mixed group, you could run both Bible activities simultaneously, so that the young people all get challenged on an appropriate level.

After each event, it's important to have a debrief and pray through some of the issues (positive or negative) that have arisen. Evaluate the event – what worked well? What went down badly? Do you need to change the way you do things for next time?

# PLANNING YOUR DECATHLON PROGRAMME

## PLANNING DECATHLON

When you start to think about using *Decathlon* as a whole programme, there are some big issues that need to be tackled:

### Define your aims

The broad aims of *Decathlon* are on page 5, but each individual programme will have its own specific aims. *Decathlon* can provide a manageable, creative and fun way of reaching out to the young people of your neighbourhood with the good news of Jesus. It can provide an excellent opportunity to blow any misconceptions away and to reveal to them a God who loves them passionately. Your aims will affect the way you use the *Decathlon* material – for assemblies? As a club programme during the school holidays? As part of an existing regular event?

Here are some aims which you might choose for your programme:

- To attract new young people to join your Sunday groups or other youth activities.
- To develop your leaders' gifts and experience.
- To present the gospel to young people who've never heard it.
- To provide an opportunity for young people to make an initial or further commitment to follow Jesus.
- To get to know the young people in your church.
- To provide a project to encourage your church to work together.
- To establish links with the young people's families.
- To encourage cooperation with other churches or groups in your area.
- To launch an ongoing youth group based on the *Decathlon* theme.

Any or all of these aims may be appropriate, but you'll have to decide what you want *Decathlon* to achieve in your situation. If you have several aims, you'll need to decide which are the most important. You'll also need to evaluate *Decathlon* afterwards, to see if you met your aims. Decide now how you'll do that. How will you measure success?

### The young people

Once you have set your aims, you'll be able to make other key decisions such as:

*Who will you invite to Decathlon?*
Do your aims relate to the young people outside your church, or those already involved in it?

How many young people do you want to involve? If your main aim is to get to know the young people better, you might need to restrict numbers. On the other hand, if you want to present the gospel to young people who haven't heard it, you may want as many as possible to attend.

What age range(s) do you want to target with *Decathlon*? Do you want to cater for an age range that is well represented in your groups, or one that isn't?

*When will you run your programme, and for how long?*

If you're running a *Decathlon* programme during the school holidays, you'll need to fix the dates early enough for potential leaders to take it into account when they book their holidays. It is also essential that the dates do not clash with other events in the area, activities already booked at your potential premises, holidays organised by local schools, holidays/camps for local Boys' Brigade, Girls' Brigade, Guide or Scout groups, carnivals or local events taking place in your area.

**Legal requirements**

Once again, if you're running a *Decathlon* programme during the school holidays, there are various legal requirements you will need to be familiar with and conform to as you prepare. These include having a safeguarding children policy in place, providing adequate space in your venue, meeting adult to young person ratios, and insurance. To obtain up-to-date information on all of these requirements, Scripture Union's website for running children's holiday clubs gives good, up-to-date advice: visit www.scriptureunion.org.uk/holidayclubs. Most of the information is applicable to young people as well as children (as most of the legislation applies to all under-18s).

**Finances**

However you plan to use *Decathlon*, you'll need to consider your financial resources. Work out what you'll need money for. Examples might include:

- refreshments
- photocopying/printing costs
- hire of premises
- hire of equipment such as a video projector
- prizes or presents for the young people

Do you need to do some fund-raising? Or will you charge a small fee for young people to attend a *Decathlon* event that runs for longer than an hour? Research shows that in many cases, making a charge for a children's holiday club has no effect on the number of children who come. Indeed, some parents may value a club they have had to pay for more highly than something that is free. The same might be true for youth activities.

**Publicity**

If you're running *Decathlon* as a special club or event, you'll need to think about how you'll publicise your programme to attract the young people you want to appeal to.

There is material available from CPO to help you with this. See the inside back cover for details. Here are some things to consider:

*Posters and flyers*

Use these to advertise your *Decathlon* programme.

*Letters and forms*

How about sending a letter, invitation card, email or text to every young person your church has contact with? (Bear in mind the safeguarding issues this raises.) Or you might distribute letters to all the young people in your area, maybe through the local schools. Your letter could enclose an application/registration form to be returned to you. You may also need a follow-up letter, which will enclose a consent/medical form.

*Press releases*

This kind of programme provides the kind of story that local papers love to cover. By getting a story in the press, you'll increase the appeal of your *Decathlon* programme and show that the church(es) involved are reaching out into your local community. By mentioning Urban Saints, YFC and Scripture Union, it increases our awareness, which ultimately allows us to improve resources. If you have a good relationship with your local press, then make contact in the usual way and inform them of your event. If this is something you have never considered, press release templates are available on the Scripture Union holiday club website (www. scriptureunion.org.uk/holidayclubs) – adapt them to fit your programme.

*Prayer cards/bookmarks*

It is important to keep your church informed about your event. Prayer cards or prayer bookmarks can help your church members pray for your programme – before, during and after your *Decathlon* event.

## PLAN IN DETAIL

In whatever context you plan to use *Decathlon*, you'll need to tailor the resources to fit your circumstances. A chart is also provided on page 12 to help you.

### Assemblies

In an assembly, you only have a short amount of time, so you may have to adapt both the sports activity and the talk to fit the duration of the session. Also, the facilities the school has available will dictate what you can do with the material (particularly the sports activity). However, do strive to make these activities work in your context, as they will provide positive memories of Christians, their local church and, most importantly, the message of Jesus Christ.

### 'God slots' in a youth group

If you plan to use the *Decathlon* material as teaching slots in an otherwise 'social' youth group, then you have a bit more freedom than if you were doing these in school. You could play the sports activity during the whole youth group, and then use the talk to refer back to it. You could also adapt some of the other resources in each event, particularly the introductory activities, to do during the rest of the evening, so that your theme stretches informally across the whole youth group time.

### Evening cell groups or Sunday morning groups

Choose the majority of your activities from the *Resources for 11 to 14s* or *Resources for 14 to 18s* sections (according to the ages of your group). For each event, choose the Bible activity first, then an introductory activity and response that goes with what you want to achieve through the Bible activity.

Try to fit in the sports activity from the Assembly/Basic talk outline so that your group get to think about the sport and the values behind it (though you don't need to do the talk, as you'll be exploring this theme through other activities). If you are short on time, do the sports activity instead of an introductory activity.

Be ready to adapt your programme should one activity overrun (or not last as long as you thought). If you are overrunning, make sure that you complete the Bible activity, as this is the main time that the young people will encounter God and what he wants to say to them. If you are running out of material, then you can always do the sports activity a second time!

## School-holiday programme

You may be planning to use the *Decathlon* material in the same way as a children's holiday club. Depending on how many days you're running, you'll need to select the events carefully to fit the needs of your young people. Try to choose events with aims that complement each other, and that lead your group on a path that will help them to meet and get to know God better.

For example, if you're running five two-hour sessions, you'll probably need to choose five events. However, if you are running longer sessions, you might be able to fit two events into one session. If you're running longer sessions, you'll need to think about breaking for a snack or maybe lunch. Factor these things in as you choose activities and plan your programme. You're unlikely to run short of time in a session like this, but you may need to put on extra activities to provide variety. Run some informal sports sessions, such as football or rounders, or learn to play some of the actual sport from *Decathlon*, such as goalball or archery.

## Other considerations

*Data protection*

How will you maintain the confidentiality of the information you receive on the registration forms? Make sure your church is registered under the Data Protection Act. Visit **www. informationcommissioner.gov.uk** and click on 'Data protection'.

*Accidents*

Make sure you have at least one person appointed as a first-aider with a current first aid certificate and access to an up-to-date first aid kit. The whole team should know who is responsible for first aid. You will also need an accident book to record any incidents. This is essential in the event of an insurance claim. The matter should be recorded, however small, along with details of the action taken. Visit **www.rospa.co.uk** for other health and safety information. There is a sample risk assessment on page 78.

*Fire procedures*

It is essential that the whole team knows emergency procedures, including fire exits and assembly points, and where to access a telephone in case of emergency. Ensure you keep all fire exits clear.

*Prayer team*

Make sure you have a team of people committed to pray throughout the preparation and the programme itself. Keep the whole church well informed too. The prayer team should keep on praying for the young people in the club in the months after your *Decathlon* programme finishes.

# DECATHLON PLANNING CHART

Use this quick chart to help you choose the material to fit your context.

## ASSEMBLY

Use the Assembly/Basic talk outline. Adapt the sports activity and the talk to suit the length of time you have and the facilities provided by the school.

## GOD SLOT

Use the Assembly/Basic talk outline as the God slot itself, but play the sports activity throughout the club time.

Adapt some of the other activities (particularly the introductory activities) from that event to do during the whole club time.

## CELL/SUNDAY GROUP

Do the sports activity from the Assembly/Basic talk outline. Then choose an:
– Introductory activity
– Bible
– Response

If short on time, drop the introductory activity.

## SCHOOL-HOLIDAY PROGRAMME

Do the sports activity from the Assembly/Basic talk outline. Then choose an:
– Introductory activity
– Bible
– Response

Augment the programme with other sports activities to provide variety.

Depending on the length of each session, match two events to do during one session.

Factor in break and meal times, if necessary.

Consider the need for free time too.

# OTHER DECATHLON EVENTS

Whether you're using *Decathlon* in school assemblies or as part of a summer programme, there are several other events you can schedule to carry on the *Decathlon* feel and bring young people (and potentially their families) together for longer times of fun and activities. The idea of these events is that they are more social, but you could include some Christian input if you feel it is appropriate to your situation.

This may be an ideal time to invite people into your church (especially if they have never been in your building before). But if your building isn't suitable, then look around for appropriate places you can use. Depending on your circumstances, a neutral venue may be the best option.

## OPENING CEREMONY

An opening ceremony is a good way to introduce the themes and sports that you'll be exploring during your *Decathlon* programme. As well as young people, you could invite families along to this event. Provide the facilities to play some of the games from *Decathlon* and either leave them open for people to play at any time, or have a programme of events in which each one is played in turn. You could provide some kind of entertainment – maybe there is a band at your church who could play a short set?

## BIG SCREEN EVENTS

If you are running *Decathlon* during the year of the Olympic or Commonwealth Games, take this opportunity for people to get together and watch the sporting events on a large screen. It would be worth trying to predict when Great Britain (or your home nation) will win medals and arrange your viewing for those evenings. You could also show the Opening and/ or Closing Ceremonies. You will need to check you have the right information about permission to show the events on a big screen. Contact the More than Gold website for more details of this at **www.morethangold.org.uk**. Provide appropriate food and drink for all the people who come. Beware of hygiene and allergy issues.

## SPORTS DAY AND BBQ

Put together a sports day for your young people, maybe using some of the sports and games that you have played during the *Decathlon* sessions. Provide prizes for people who do well (maybe the winners, or the ones that you feel have improved the most) – you could use some of the *Decathlon* products (see the inside back cover) as prizes.

You may wish to provide lunch or dinner as part of the day, and a barbeque is an ideal way of doing this. Make sure you have someone who has the correct food hygiene qualifications to cook for you.

## LEARNING SPECIFIC SPORTS

You might have sports clubs in your area who would be willing to come to an event to teach the young people some of the specifics of their sport. Football clubs often have a community department, employing coaches and community officers to run events in their surrounding area. You might also wish to learn something of sports, which are not as widely played, such as handball or volleyball, or a Paralympic sport, such as goalball. Indeed, learning a sport that is new to everyone means that all the young people will be starting from the same place. Make sure you provide sufficient refreshments, including plenty of water.

## AWARDS/MEDALS CEREMONY

Towards the end of your *Decathlon* programme, you could plan to give awards or medals according to what the young people have got up to at the sessions. Make this light-hearted (although, if there have been great performances, make sure you reward those!), but not condescending or mean. This could be tied to the closing ceremony and could be a place where young people are valued by you with their families present.

## CLOSING CEREMONY

The closing ceremony of a games event is often more relaxed and includes music and other entertainment slots which you could recreate in your own closing ceremony. This allows you to include young people who aren't as keen on sport, as you could incorporate music and dance items, cheerleading, presenting and reporting etc. This would be especially appropriate, as you could report back to parents/guardians, friends and family (or indeed the church!) what you have been doing, discovering and achieving.

# DECATHLON
# EVENT 1
## GOALBALL / WHO IS GOD?

### TARGET

To understand that we don't always need to see things with physical eyes to know they're real, and that the same is true of God.

### KEY PASSAGE

Luke 15:11–32 and others

### TRAINING FOR YOU

Goalball is a game for visually impaired players. It is one of the most exciting team sports in the Paralympics programme. It's used here to illustrate how we know God is real, even though we can't see him. The session is designed to be an introduction to God for those who have never met him before. Before you look at the activities, spend some time reflecting on who God is to you. Personal stories are powerful evangelistic tools, and young people will look to you for an authentic example of what a relationship with God looks like.

Spend some time praying for the young people who are going to come to your group (or those who will attend your assembly). Ask God, as you introduce young people to him, to work in their hearts and open them up to hearing more about him.

### FOR YOUNG PEOPLE OUTSIDE A CHURCH COMMUNITY

This is very much an introductory session for young people with no church background. They may be encountering God for the first time here, so you will need to be ready for their different reactions. Some may bring negative preconceptions and defensive questions, where others might be overwhelmed by God, having never heard about him before. Be sensitive to all these valid reactions, and treat them all with gentleness and respect.

### FOR CHURCH YOUNG PEOPLE

For young people with a church background, this might not be new ground, but they may have ideas of who God is that aren't biblically based, and you may need to challenge some of them. There are a couple of activities designed to stretch church young people, so try to include those in your session. However, if you have a mixed group, then you'll need to be careful with the mix of activities you choose.

**Goalball UK**
www.goalballuk.com

# ASSEMBLY/ BASIC TALK OUTLINE

Aim: to understand that we don't always need to see things with physical eyes to know they're real, and that the same is true of God.

## WHAT YOU NEED

- A soft football-sized ball that makes a sound (eg with a bell inside)
- Eye masks or blindfolds
- Two goal posts
- Pitch markings (if not using an actual pitch, ensure you can mark one out with masking tape)

## WHAT YOU DO

Create teams of three young people. The ultimate aim of the game, like football, is to score goals. In this event, however, both teams will be blindfolded and must locate the ball based on its sound. You may want to build up skills with the players before the match begins, for example, getting them used to detecting the ball's sound, getting used to its weight and the necessary force it will take to roll the ball towards the goal.

When the players are rehearsed enough to play, each team should be positioned in front of their own goal. The aim is for each team, in turn, to score by rolling the ball into the opposition's goal, while the opposition attempts to block the ball with their bodies. It is then the opposition's turn to try to score, and so on, with the ball going back and forth. Keep a track of the scores and award prizes to the winning team. (If running this with a class, you may like to extend this into mini-matches with multiple teams, or rotate teams so that everybody has a turn at playing.)

Go on to say that there are some things in life that are perfectly real, even if we can't see them. In the game, it wasn't possible to see the ball – but we learned to recognise it by hearing it, helping us to locate it and use it to play the game.

One of the big questions that people often ask is whether or not God exists. A lot of people think that God can't exist, on the basis that they can't see him with their eyes. If he's real, surely he should show himself. But is that reason enough to discount God? Christians would say that even if you cannot see him with your actual physical eyesight, you are able to see him if your 'spiritual' eyes are switched on. Just like in the game it was necessary to find other ways of 'seeing' the ball while your eyes weren't being used, so people see God in ways such as in the evidence of the beautiful world around them, or they feel a special presence around them which they believe to be God. Many people claim to hear God speaking to them, giving them messages through his special book, the Bible, or through other people talking to them about something that had been on their mind, or even just in their own quiet time at home or in church.

In the Bible, God says that people will seek him and find him when they look for him with their 'whole heart' (Jeremiah 29:13). In other words, he wants people to see and meet him in a special way. It's up to us to get looking!

# RESOURCES FOR 11 TO 14S

## WHO IS IT?

**Introductory activity**
**For all groups**
**10 minutes**

Aim: to introduce the theme of who God really is.

### WHAT YOU NEED
• Pictures of celebrities
• Sticky tape
• Sheets of paper

### WHAT YOU DO
Before this session, cut out pictures of celebrities from magazines. Using some blank sheets of paper (the same size as the pictures), cut holes in parts of the blank paper and then stick them over the pictures of the celebrities. It should be that the pictures are partially covered up, and that there are glimpses of the picture through the blank paper. Number each picture. (You could adapt this idea for an assembly by using PowerPoint.)

Sit everyone down together and pass round the partial pictures of the celebrities for people to try and guess who each one is. Alternatively stick the pictures round the walls for everyone to wander round and look at. Give people paper and pens and ask them to write down who they think the celebrities are from the glimpses they can see through the holes in the blank pieces of paper.

After a few minutes, collect the pictures in and unmask each celebrity.

Say that today they will be thinking about who God is, even though everyone probably has their own ideas. However, as we look at what the Bible says about God, we will get a much clearer picture of exactly who he is rather than just glimpses of him.

## PICTURE GOD

**Introductory activity**
**For all groups**
**5 minutes**

Aim: to start to think about who God is and to introduce the idea that we can never know everything about God.

### WHAT YOU NEED
• Puzzle-shaped pieces of paper
• Pens or pencils

### WHAT YOU DO
Before the session, cut up a large (A1) sheet of paper into jigsaw-shaped pieces. Put a small number in the top right-hand corner of each piece so it can easily be reassembled.

Give each person or a small group of people (depending on the number of young people) a piece of the puzzle to write down anything they feel is relevant to the question 'Who is God?'

If you have a very large group ask for volunteers to shout out answers and get other leaders to write up their answers onto the different pieces. In this way you can have several people writing at the same time.

As people come to an end with their ideas, start to piece the puzzle together. Read out a few of the suggestions. Then say that during this session they will be thinking a little more about who God is, and whilst all the gaps in the puzzle will never be completely filled, at least there may be a few more ideas by the end.

## PICTURES OF GOD

**Bible**
**For all groups**
**10 minutes**

Aim: to look at three biblical pictures of who God is.

### WHAT YOU NEED
• Bibles

### WHAT YOU DO
The Bible is full of clues as to who God is. From beginning to end there are countless different pictures and ideas, all of which help us get a better understanding. But because God is so much more than our human minds can cope with, we can never have a complete picture. In a way, this makes the Christian faith journey so interesting and different

cause it seems that the more we get
know about God the more there is to
cover – no one will ever get to the end
knowing who God is. Here are three
tures from the Bible which explain a
e about who God is:

epherd
the first picture, we see a loving
epherd taking care of his flock of sheep.
ad Psalm 23:1–4 (NLT). Ask the young
ople what they learn of the Shepherd
m these verses. Draw out that he
ows them all individually and he looks
er all his sheep's needs, providing them
th good grazing and water, leading
em and protecting them at all times.
u could also look at John 10:11–15, to
pand on this image of the shepherd,
rticularly to show that the shepherd is
en willing to die for his sheep.

ther
e second picture is that of a loving
ther. Many children today struggle with
e idea that a father can be totally loving
d completely wanting the best for
em. This is the picture that Jesus gives
of his loving Father God.

In Jesus' picture of a loving father,
found in Luke 15:11–32, we see that he
will never hold onto any of his children
against their will. If they want to walk
away from him he allows this, but he
longs for them to come back home and
call him Father again. How does the
Father greet the son on his return? What
would you have done, if you had been in
his shoes? What does this tell us about his
feelings for his children?

**Holiness**
The third picture is found in the book
of Isaiah in the Bible. It's a dramatically
different picture to the shepherd or
loving father. In this account, the prophet
Isaiah sees God in all his holiness, purity
and power. Read Isaiah 6:1–5. Ask the
young people how they would have
felt in Isaiah's shoes. Why did Isaiah
feel so 'impure'? Have they ever had
an experience of feeling very small or
insignificant in front of God's holiness?
Get them to share their stories and think
about what God's holiness is like.

(If you think that your group of young
people from outside a church community
would struggle with looking at three
pictures of God, concentrate on the
'Father' image of God.)

# PICTURE CONNECTION
**Response**
**For all groups**
**5 minutes**

Aim: to encourage the young people to
reflect more on who God is and to allow
them time to respond.

## WHAT YOU NEED
• Pens and paper
• Worship music and the means to play it

## WHAT YOU DO
Ask the young people to sit quietly and
reflect on the three pictures of God they
have just heard about. Ask them to think
about which one they feel the most
connection with: God the Good Shepherd
looking out for them and caring for them;
God the loving Father welcoming them
home and giving them a hug, whatever
state they're in; or God, all holy and
awesome.

Ask them to write or draw their responses
– perhaps a simple sentence or a prayer to
God – and to take these away with them.
You might also like to play a song related
to one of the pictures. If appropriate,
close this time with a prayer.

If you have a group for which this kind of
response is new, then give them guidance
by providing emotions as stimuli: write
down words like 'excited', 'nervous',
'bored', 'happy' on slips of paper and ask
your group to choose some words which
describe how they feel at the moment.

# RESOURCES FOR 14 TO 18S

## DESCRIBE ME!

**Introductory activity**
**For all groups**
**15 minutes**

Aim: to help young people understand that there are many aspects to the character of God.

### WHAT YOU NEED

• Post-it® notes
• Pens

### WHAT YOU DO

Invite your group to cover one of the other members in Post-it® notes! Ask for a volunteer to stand in the middle of the group and hand out pens and Post-it® notes to the rest of the group.

Those with the Post-it® notes have two minutes to come up with as many ways of describing the person in the middle as possible. They should write each description on a Post-it® and then stick it to them.

Make sure that all the descriptions are clean and kind, and make sure the person in the middle is happy with what's happening!

Explain that just as we have many aspects to our personalities, God also has many facets to his character. Because of this, it is not always easy to respond to the question 'Who is God?' with a straightforward answer. Tell them that you are going to spend the remainder of the session exploring the character of God further.

## CHIP OFF THE OLD BLOCK

**Bible**
**For all groups**
**10 minutes (or 20 minutes for the church-group extension)**

Aim: to learn more about God by looking at the person of Jesus Christ.

### WHAT YOU NEED

• Bibles
• Study Bibles, concordances etc (optional)
• Flip-chart paper
• Pens

Begin by reading the following verses with your group:
• Hebrews 1:3
• John 14:9
• Colossians 1:15

Explain that by looking at Jesus we can learn more about God's character – Jesus is the perfect image of an invisible God. Split your group into smaller groups and ask them to come up with their 'Top three characteristics of Jesus'. Hand out the papers and pens and move around each group, helping them.

Give the group the time they need to complete this and then ask them to report back to the rest of the group. Write up the different characteristics they report back with – some will be the same as the other groups. Once each group has reported back, refer back to the verses. What does it mean that Jesus is the 'image of the invisible God', the 'exact representation of God'? When Jesus said 'if you've seen me you've seen the father', what was he getting at?

We're trying to get the group to click that Jesus IS God! We know what Jesus was like – we can read about him. If we can see what Jesus was like, we can see a bit of what God is like!

To challenge church groups, tell the group that for each characteristic, they need to come up with a story or example of Jesus demonstrating that characteristic. This isn't easy, so provide study Bibles, concordances etc and give as much help as you can.

## WHO DO YOU SAY I AM?

**Bible**
**For church groups**
**10 minutes**

Aim: to help the young people to think about whether they believe in an angry or a loving God, and what they should do to find out more.

### WHAT YOU NEED

• A Bible
• Flip-chart paper and marker pen

## WHAT YOU DO

Before the session, go through this talk script and make it your own, adapting and adding to it, as suits your group:

It is natural to ask questions in life. If you're unsure how to do something at school or college, you ask the teacher or lecturer what to do. If you go to a new place and don't know where you are going, you ask for directions. It is part of life and learning to ask questions.

People have so many questions to ask about God and who he is. They want to know why he lets bad things happen in the world. They want to know why there is suffering and death, and why people hate each other and fight in wars.

Invariably, people ask questions about God when they are hurt or angry. They don't tend to shout out to God when they are happy and things are going well. Everyone has their own idea of who they think God is. Some people think that he is an angry God who does not care for us, but instead wants to punish us and make us suffer. Others believe that God is a God of love who wants to be a part of our lives.

The Bible tells us that God is many things. Psalm 103 particularly talks about his love and faithfulness for us. (Ask some young people to read this, or read it out loud yourself, all the way through. Then get them to call out phrases, or words from the psalm which describe God's character. If possible, write these up on a flip chart.)

What is the 'big' picture of God that this psalm leaves us with? It's an overwhelmingly positive picture of a God who is loving, forgiving, compassionate, faithful and just – very different from the angry and vengeful God that he is sometimes made out to be!

Sometimes we can spend too much time worrying about what to call God and what he is, rather than who he is and the relationship that we can have with him. It doesn't matter what name we call him. All that matters, is who he is. God is love and compassion, and he wants to play a part in our lives. He wants to help us and support us when we are down and struggling. He wants to celebrate with us and share our joy when we succeed or are happy.

Doesn't this sound like someone that you would like to know and to be a part of your life? If you believe that he is an angry, judgemental God, it is quite understandable that you may not want to have anything to do with him. However, if he is this loving and great God that so many people believe in, it is surely worth looking into it all a bit more and getting to know him better.

## ANGRY? HAPPY? INTERESTED?

**Response**
**For all groups**
**5 minutes**

Aim: to give the young people some time to reflect on what they have learned and how they feel about it.

## WHAT YOU DO

Ask the group to think about what they have learned in today's session. Explain that the things you have said may make them feel one of three things (or possibly all of them!):
*Angry* – you may have made them feel really cross by telling them that God loves them and wants to get to know them more. They may be finding life hard work and this just isn't what they want to hear.
*Happy* – everything you told them is either something they believe already and needed it to be re-affirmed or may be totally new to them, but they feel really happy about the idea that God cares for them.
*Interested* – they may also feel angry and happy as well as this, because people who are interested to find out more about God have many questions that they need answering as they seek to find answers.

Ask the group to spend a few minutes quietly thinking about how they feel about God. If they want to, they could try talking to God silently to voice their feelings. When they have had a few minutes, draw the activity to a close by inviting them to come and see you if they want to discuss how this session has made them feel.

# DECATHLON EVENT 2

## VOLLEYBALL/WE ARE PART OF GOD'S PLAN

### TARGET

To see that we are not bouncing aimlessly through life – God loves us and has got a clear direction for our lives.

### KEY PASSAGE

Ephesians 2:1–10

### TRAINING FOR YOU

You may not have thought much about this recently, but what does the cross mean to you? Rescue? Sacrifice? Victory? Something else? How would you explain that to a young person with no experience of Christianity. This session allows young people to explore the fact that we are all part of God's plan, because he wants all of us to become his friends. He sent Jesus to put things right between us and him. Spend some time thinking about what that means to you and get yourself ready to explain it all to your group.

### FOR YOUNG PEOPLE OUTSIDE A CHURCH COMMUNITY

Young people with no experience of Christianity may not have any experience of the idea that God has a plan for people, and that he made such a sacrifice so that we could be his friends. They could react either way to this story, and so, as in the last session, you need to be ready for all reactions.

### FOR CHURCH YOUNG PEOPLE

Despite being part of a church community, these young people may not have understood properly the cross and what it means. You may need to help them experience it afresh. To help them, you might want to check out *Top Tips on Explaining the cross* (see below for details). Alternatively, you may just need to refresh their basic understanding and help them move further in their relatioship with God.

For advice on how to explain to young people what Jesus did on the cross, check out *Top Tips on Explaining the Cross* by Helen Franklin, Steve Hutchinson and Robert Willoughby (SU).

**English Volleyball Association**
www.volleyballengland.org
**Scottish Volleyball Association**
www.scottishvolleyball.org
**Volleyball Wales**
www.volleyballwales.org
**Northern Ireland Volleyball**
www.nivb.com
**UK Beach Volleyball**
www.beachvolleyball.org.uk

£3.50
9781844273300

# ASSEMBLY/
# BASIC TALK OUTLINE

Aim: to see that we are not bouncing aimlessly through life – God loves us and has got a clear direction for our lives.

## WHAT YOU NEED

- Hairdryers
- Balloon(s)
- Volleyball net (or equivalent)
- A blanket
- Extension leads as appropriate
- Strong sticky tape

## WHAT YOU DO

Before the session, set up the net volleyball-style. Tape the extension leads down so that each player can use a hairdryer without tripping over any electical wiring (you will need to keep an eye on this health and safety issue during the game). Invite a few volunteers to hold the blanket between the base of the net and the floor.

Invite between two and four volunteers to play. These should each have a hairdryer. Use a balloon as a volleyball and serve it above the net. Rather than hitting the balloon over the net, the young people need to blow it over using the hairdryer. (Put the hairdryers on the coolest setting to prevent bursting the balloons from the heat!) If the balloon hits the blanket, the team on the other side wins the point. You can make this more challenging by adding in more balloons as you go.

When the game is finished make these points:

Sometimes we can feel as if our lives are a bit like the balloons in our game. They don't have any particular purpose or direction; they just get blown along by chance or circumstance. Even our best plans and ideas are easily messed up and things don't work out. So what is the point of being here? Is there one?

The Bible teaches that there is a point. It paints a picture of a God who is not just real, not just all-powerful and all-knowing, but one who is also all-loving. He isn't a distant God who made the world but doesn't have much interest in what it's doing now. He's a God who continues to be involved, making us, knowing us and loving us. The picture of God, found in the book of Psalms, is one who saw us in our mother's tummies – even before she knew we were there (Psalm 139); who knows how many hairs are on our heads (Luke 12:7); who even knows how many days we are going to be alive (Psalm 39:4). And the Bible teaches that the God who knows us this well has a plan for our lives – and he wants us to live so that we can make the very most out of it.

We are not here by accident. Neither is any of us simply a product of what happens to us. We all have one life to live and it's our choice whether or not we're going to work out what the best thing to do with that life is. The Bible helps us to understand who the Maker is and how we should live his way – will you give it a go?

# RESOURCES FOR 11 TO 14S

## WHO IS IT?
**Introductory activity**
**For all groups**
**10 minutes**

Aim: to discover the differences between living God's way and the world's way.

### WHAT YOU NEED
• Two large sheets of paper
• Marker pens

### WHAT YOU DO
Stick two big sheets of paper to a wall. On one, write GOD'S VALUES and on the other, WORLD'S VALUES. (To keep the volleyball theme going, you could portray these as two halves of a volleyball court, with a net in between.) Hand out some marker pens and ask the group to come and write up on the sheets of paper values that are seen as Christian/godly ones, and values that our culture tries to put on us.

Hopefully, some of the following (and more) will be listed:
*God's values* – serving others, not looking after number one, loving God, obeying God, looking after other people, giving to the needy, etc.
*World's values* – sex, loads of money, drink, etc.
Chat about how the world – our society – might want you to believe that the main aim of life is to earn loads of money, sleep with whoever you like whenever you like, drink to excess and prove how much fun you can have in the process, party hard, etc. But God's values are different. So we have a choice to do what all our mates seem to be doing, or to go against the flow, and to live our lives God's way.

This doesn't mean that God wants to spoil your fun – in fact he wants to give you the best life possible. For example, God doesn't want us to sleep around. Why do you think that is? See if the group come up with some ideas. Then go on to say that God's best is to see sex as something shared between a husband and a wife in a loving, committed relationship – it's not something that should mess us up emotionally or physically.

Ask the group to:
• make a list of their core values – how they think they should live their lives.
• write down how they think God wants them to live – does this differ at all from their list?

---

## IN THE DARK
**Bible**
**For all groups**
**10 minutes**

Aim: to discover that God has not left people in the dark to just get on with life – he's given us the Bible to show us how to live. And when we mess up, God forgives us and wants us to keep going.

### WHAT YOU NEED
• Paper and pens

### WHAT YOU DO
Give everyone a sheet of paper and a pen and ask them to close their eyes, or turn the lights out to make the room dark. The task is to get everyone to draw what you say – in the dark!

Read out the following instructions:
– Draw a circle and then some lines coming from the circle – this is the sun.
– Now draw the shape of a house.
– On the roof draw a chimney.
– The house has four windows and curtains.
– Draw a front door in the centre of the house.
– Outside the house there are a couple of trees in the garden.
– On the trees there are some apples.
– Above the house are some birds.
– Parked by one side of the house is a car.

Turn on the lights or get everyone to open their eyes and see how well the pictures have turned out. Share with the group how hard it is to draw in the dark.

Sometimes as Christians we feel as if we are in the dark, without real guidance, but God has given us the Bible to show us how to live his way. God has not left us in the dark. Christians are not perfect. We do and will mess up while we are alive on earth. Thankfully, God knows this and that is why we are reliant on God's grace – his favour.

Read Ephesians 2:1–10. When a young child falls over and grazes their knee, their mum or dad picks them up and wipes them up. The reaction of the mum or dad isn't harsh or cold, but it's a reaction of love and concern for their child.

If you have a group of young people from outside a church community, ask them straight away what they think about this. Do they feel like they are 'spiritually dead'? It seems like a harsh thing to say. Gather their reactions to this. If your group has church young people, they may be more familiar with this idea, but get their initial reactions as well.

Then go on to look again at verses 4 to 10. What does the group think of this. Be ready for all kinds of responses. Try to guide the conversation round to the fact that God did not leave us without any help, but sent his Son Jesus to rescue us.

# ACT OF SERVICE

**Response**
**For all groups**
**10 minutes**

Aim: to explore the fact that the Christian lifestyle is all about living for God and not ourselves – serving other people is a way in which Christians can follow God.

## WHAT YOU NEED
• Paper
• Pens
• Envelopes
• Drinks and biscuits

## WHAT YOU DO
Being a Christian might not make us the most popular person in school/college, but one thing you can do is aim to show God to people by how you live. As a group, come up with some ideas as to how practically each person can show they are living for God in their home and their school/college.
The idea of serving others is a key Christian value – something Jesus did. Why not think through some practical 'service' ideas that people can do?

Here are some ideas. However, it would be great if the group can come up with some of their own:
• Clean your mum/dad's car without being asked
• Offer to wash the dishes – amaze your mum/dad
• Cook a meal one evening for your family
• Set up a recycling scheme in your school
• Promote Fairtrade items in school
• Say sorry to your brother or sister next time you annoy them

After chatting through some ideas (perhaps over drinks and some food, considering hygiene and allergy issues), encourage each member of the group to commit to do something so as to make a response. Do this by getting them to write their act of 'service' down on a strip of paper and then pop it into an envelope, writing their name on the envelope. Then collect the envelopes and say that in a few months the envelopes will be handed back and each person can see how they have responded.

# RESOURCES FOR 14 TO 18S

## A MAP FOR THE PERPLEXED
**Introductory activity**
**For all groups**
**15 minutes**

Aim: to encourage the young people to reflect on the direction and purpose of their life in the light of God's love.

### WHAT YOU NEED
• Large sheets of paper (A3 would be fine)
• Art materials (pens, pencils, pastels, paint, etc)

### WHAT YOU DO
This activity provides a focus for reflecting on our individual journeys. You might want to play some quiet music to encourage a reflective atmosphere. Introduce the activity by explaining that you are going to be using the materials provided to make a 'map' of your life.

Some things you might want to include on your map are:
• your current location (where are you in your life now?)
• where you have come from
• the path you took to get to where you are now
• the journey ahead
• destinations or resting places along the way

But essentially, it is up to the individual to decide what the map should look like – after all, everyone is different! As you are making your map, you might want to think about some of these points (you could write these on a board or on the wall where they will be visible:

• Even when we have spent a lot of time planning a journey, we might decide to change our route. What sort of things interest you enough to make you alter your course?
• Sometimes we encounter obstacles along a route. How do obstacles affect your journey? Do you become discouraged, or look for another way round?
• Long journeys can be very tiring. Do you take time to rest? How do you seek refreshment when life tires you out?

Allow 15 minutes for your group to make their maps. Finish the activity by reading John 14:4–6 together. God is not just interested in our journey – he *is* our journey! Encourage group members to talk about their own maps, and where they might have experienced God's guidance.

## SEEDS OF LIFE
**Bible**
**For all groups**
**10 minutes**

Aim: to bring to life the images of seeds and growth that Jesus often used when talking about the kingdom of God.

### WHAT YOU NEED
• Small plant pots
• Marker pens
• Potting compost
• Packet of seeds*
• Trowels
• Newspaper to protect the work area

*You should pick a seed which is large enough to handle easily. Good choices are broad beans or runner beans.

### WHAT YOU DO
Begin by reading Matthew 13:31,32. Give each person a seed, a plant pot and a marker pen. Then read the following instructions:

– Hold the seed in your hand. Look at it carefully. Examine its texture and shape.
– It is such a small thing, and yet from this, God can bring a beautiful plant which provides us with food.
– Think for a minute about your life. It may seem small and insignificant. It may not look like much at the moment. But from you, God can bring forth great things.
– Your seed needs the right conditions to grow. Put some compost in your pot, and plant the seed in it. The soil will keep it warm. Water and light will encourage it to grow.
– Now think about yourself. What do you need to grow? Think about the physical things.
– What about other things you need: emotional needs? Spiritual needs?

24

Now read Ephesians 2:1–10. The seed in their hand is 'dead', but given the right circumstances it 'comes alive'. We were 'dead', but in the right circumstances of God's love, we come alive.

Read Mark 10:27. Write the words 'all things are possible with God' around your plant pot to remind you of what God can do with your life. As you look after your plant and watch it grow, think about what God is doing in your life day by day.

## THE BEST WAY
**Bible**
**For church groups**
**20 minutes**

Aim: to explore following God's plan for our lives and how we get distracted.

## WHAT YOU NEED
• Paper and pens

## WHAT YOU DO
Ask your group this question: 'How can we live God's best life?'

Have each of them write a brief answer on a slip of paper (no more than five words). Collect the answers and share them with the group. How many of them involve an action on the part of the individual?

When we think about 'living God's best life' what springs to mind? For many of us, the first thing we think will be along the lines of 'I must try to be a better person.'

We are so used to putting ourselves at the centre of things that we assume immediately that it is an activity on our part which is required.

Actually, the first step to living God's best life is to draw closer to him. God created us, and the world we live in, with great care. In his original plan, he provided for us everything we need. Because of sin and disobedience, we now find it harder to receive his blessings – but they are still there for us. His ultimate plan for us and for the planet we live on, is to restore us to the perfection of his original design.

Ask the group what they know about King David. Write those thoughts down on the paper and then read 2 Samuel 11 with the group. If the group has only heard of the positive things about David, this story may be a surprise. How did David not live God's way in this story? Go through the different ways David followed his own desires and tried to cover his tracks.

Explain that David was God's chosen king and was very close to God. What do the young people think about how this story fits into the rest of David's life? You might chat about how easy it is to slip from God's way. Discuss what more we can do to follow the best life? Is it about what we do? Or about the relationship with God we have?

## THINGS THAT GET IN THE WAY
**Response**
**For all groups**
**15 minutes**

Aim: to provide an opportunity for the group to share with each other the things they find difficult in living God's best life, and to allow them to pray for each other.

## WHAT YOU NEED
• Maps from 'A map for the perplexed'

## WHAT YOU DO
Ask the group to get into groups of two or three, preferably with people they feel comfortable sharing with. If they don't feel comfortable with other members of the group maybe they could share with a leader.

Ask them to look at the maps they made earlier in the session and to identify those things that get in the way of, or pull them away from, living God's best life. Ask your young people to share one thing with the rest of their small group.

Go on to ask the groups to pray together (bearing in mind that some young people will be unused to this or uncomfortable with it) about those things that pull us away from God's life. Ask for God's help to carry on following him.

# DECATHLON EVENT 3

## ARCHERY / WHY DID JESUS DIE?

### TARGET

To realise that, though we don't always get things right, God wants to give us a new start.

### KEY PASSAGE

Romans 5:1–11

### TRAINING FOR YOU

This session moves the young people on from the previous one, to think more clearly about what Jesus did on the cross. Your story will be particularly powerful here – an authentic outworking of being made right with God, as seen in your life, will speak loudly to young people from both within and outside your church community. Spend some time prayerfully reading Romans 5:1–11 and reflecting on what this means to you. What stories from your life might speak of the grace and mercy God, as shown in Jesus' sacrifice? As last session, you might want to read through *Top Tips on Explaining the cross* (SU, see page 19). This will help you think through, in more detail, what the cross means to you.

### FOR YOUNG PEOPLE OUTSIDE A CHURCH COMMUNITY

How might a young person from outside your church community feel to be told that God wants to be their friend? If you have run Events 1 and 2 already with your group, you should have started to build up good relationships with any young people new to your group. Think about them now. What would their reaction be to God wanting to be their friend? For the facebook generation, being a friend can be a much more throwaway concept than the friendship that God offers – you will need to help young people differentiate between different levels of friendship to understand a friendship with God.

### FOR CHURCH YOUNG PEOPLE

You may have a mix of young people already in your church – from those who have begun to own and work out their faith to those whose faith is one that is experienced through or shared with others, without the young person fully owning it themselves. You will need to pitch this session knowing where your young people are at. Challenge those who own their faith to move forward with Christ; nurture those who have questions and help them explore what Jesus did on the cross for themselves.

Archery GB
www.archerygb.org

# ASSEMBLY/ BASIC TALK OUTLINE

Aim: to realise that, though we don't always get things right, God wants to give us a new start.

## WHAT YOU NEED

- Spoons
- Toilet tissue
- Large target board (like the ones used in archery)
- Blindfolds
- A bowl of water
- Cover-up equipment (such as plastic dust sheets, available cheaply from DIY stores)

## WHAT YOU DO

Set up your target and spread your cover-up equipment around to avoid any mess. This is a messy game, but young people will remember it and it will form a starting point for conversation about the activity at a later date.

Invite teams of two to four young people to take part. Team members take it in turns to be blindfolded and spun round. They use their spoons to launch toilet tissue pellets (rolled up toilet tissue dipped in water) towards the target – although they could go anywhere! In order to save time and to make pellets as effective as possible, invite other members of the team to produce pellets for their blindfolded team mates as the game goes on. (It may be a good idea to set time limits for each team member and run the game as a time trial.)

We live in a world that encourages us to set targets for ourselves and our achievements. But is it always possible to live up to them? Sometimes we try to be good people but we end up messing up – getting angry with people, letting other people down, saying things which upset others. It can lead us to feel bad about ourselves and feel like a failure, not to mention hurting other people as a result.

The Bible teaches that God made us to live good lives, where we love him and other people perfectly. But people find it impossible to live his way. Like in our game, we fail to hit this target. This 'missing the mark' is what the Bible calls sin, and it is a huge problem for our world. It messes up people's relationship with God and with other people. The Bible describes a lot of the major problems on planet Earth as a result of people's sin, and every single person has a part to play in adding to these problems.

God's big solution to the problem was sending Jesus into the world. Christians believe that Jesus was God himself who came to earth to die on the cross. The Bible says that when Jesus died, he took away the sin of the world. This means that anybody who turns to God can now be forgiven for all the wrong things they have done. God himself will come to live with them, changing them into the people God always intended them to be by the power of his Holy Spirit. We may not be able to hit the mark ourselves, but God himself is now the one throwing the pellets!

(For a video illustration, use 'Why did Jesus die?' from the exploRE resource – see www.explore-tv.co.uk.)

# RESOURCES FOR 11 TO 14S

## HANDS
**Introductory activity**
**For all groups**
**15 minutes**

Aim: to start thinking about the wrong things we do, and how they are a barrier to a friendship with God.

### WHAT YOU NEED
• Archery gloves (available cheaply online)
• Paper and pens

### WHAT YOU DO
Show the archery glove you've brought with you. Let the young people try it on and get some feedback on what is unusual about it. Then give everyone a sheet of paper and ask them to either draw round their hands or draw an archery glove. On these hands, they are to write down all the different things they have done wrong. So if they have ever told a lie, ever taken anything that wasn't theirs (including not giving back borrowed property), ever been rude or unkind, or used a swear word, etc they could write these on their hand(s).

Reassure them that they are the only ones who are going to read what's on these paper hands. But they are to imagine, for a moment, that all that's been written on the paper hands, is in reality written on their own hands for everyone to see.

Who would want to shake their hands or hold their hands, if they could see all the wrong things? They might be afraid

something would rub off onto them. God is perfect and holy and he cannot allow anything dirty or imperfect close to him because that would compromise his own purity. So what can we do about all the stuff on our hands? How can we make them clean and white? Listen to a few suggestions and then say that God does have a solution; it involves a cross and some nails through the hands of a perfect man.

(If you plan to do the Response section 'Nails', then save the hands for that activity.)

## WHY?
**Introductory activity**
**For all groups**
**5 minutes**

Aim: to encourage the young people to start thinking about why Jesus died on the cross – and specifically why he chose to do this.

### WHAT YOU DO
Split the group into pairs and ask them to discuss each of these questions in turn. Give them a few minutes to do this and invite them to give feedback on each question after they have discussed it:
• Why would someone be willing to leave the people and places they loved for ever?
• Why would someone be prepared to give up their future for the sake of someone else's future?

• Why would someone be prepared to die for someone else?

Now ask the question:
• Why would someone allow himself to be put to death in the way in which only the worst criminals were killed and in the most painful way imaginable, even though he had committed no crime or done anything wrong?

Give the young people some time to think about this question, then move on to the Bible activity.

## NO GREATER LOVE
**Bible**
**For all groups**
**10 minutes**

Aim: to realise that, though we don't always get things right, God wants to give us a new start.

### WHAT YOU NEED
• Bibles
• Archery targets drawn on large sheets of paper
• Marker pens

### WHAT YOU DO
Read Romans 1:28–32 together. Give out the large sheets of paper and ask the young people to write down all the bad things people do. They should try and write the 'more serious' things at the centre of the target and those 'less serious' things towards the edge.

Chat together about why these things might make our lives worse. What are the effects of some of these things on our lives? You might talk about hurt, embarrassment or broken relationships. Depending on the make up of your group, you'll have some different responses. Do the young people see the things they do wrong as being 'wrong'? Even when no one gets hurt?

Then explain that these things also damage our relationship with God. He wants us to be his friend, but he cannot ignore the bad things we do, or pretend not to see them. How does this make the group feel?

Now read Romans 5:1–11 and encourage the group to compare the attitude of the two passages (particularly verses 1 to 5). One is negative, the other positive. What has caused this difference? Look at verses 6 to 11 again and discuss these questions:
• What does this passage say about one person dying for another?
• What do you think about that?
• What do you think of Jesus' actions – dying for us?

Read 1 Peter 2:24, and explain that God got rid of all the things we do wrong, because Jesus took the punishment in our place. Jesus said: 'The greatest love a person can show is to die for his friends' (John 15:13). In other words, the greatest act of love anyone could do is to die for another person.

You may want to leave some space in your programme for the young people to think through this. Offer to chat or pray with any young people who want to ask you more. The book *What Now?*

(SU, £2.99, 9781844275397) might be helpful here.

## NAILS

**Response**
**For all groups**
**5 minutes**

Aim: to give an opportunity for the young people to respond to Jesus dying on the cross for them.

## WHAT YOU NEED
• Two pieces of wood tied or nailed together into a cross shape
• Nails
• Hammers
• Hands from 'Hands' starting out activity
• A bowl of soapy water
• A towel
• Quiet music (optional)

## WHAT YOU DO
Place the cross in the middle of the room. Briefly explain again that, as Jesus died on the cross, he was taking on himself all the wrong things we have done or will ever do. As we hand over all the bad stuff to him and say we're sorry (and mean it), so he forgives us and makes us new and clean.

Say that anyone who wants to do this can go and nail the hands they wrote on earlier onto the cross. If they don't want others to see what they've written they can nail them on with the words facing inwards. Explain that this is a really important thing they're doing, a prayerful thing, and it should only be done if they really mean it.

Near to the cross, have a bowl of soapy water and a towel. Once the young people have nailed their hands to the cross they can wash their real hands in the water as a sign that God has forgiven them and made them clean again.

It might be good to have music playing quietly in the background and leaders on hand to talk to those who need a listening ear – especially those who don't feel ready to respond.

Make sure you supervise the nails and hammers carefully.

# RESOURCES FOR 14 TO 18S

## SUITABLE PUNISHMENT?
**Introductory activity**
**For all groups**
**10 minutes**

Aim: to get the young people to start thinking about punishments that fit crimes.

## WHAT YOU DO
Gather the group together and explain that they are going to hear several scenarios where a crime occurred. As a group, they need to decide what a suitable punishment would be for the person who committed the crime. The scenarios are as follows:

- The defendant was hungry and had no money so went into the local shop and shoplifted a bag of crisps and a can of Coke. What punishment would you give this criminal?
- The defendant was short on cash and needed money to buy some more drugs, so they followed an old lady back from the post office, cornered her, beat her up and stole all of her pension – approximately £150. What punishment would you give this criminal?
- The defendant was driving at 50 mph in a 30 mph zone and knocked a small child down. The child, although now fully recovered, was unconscious for several days and has several scars from the incident. What punishment would you give this criminal?
- The defendant annoyed a few people by challenging bad behaviour that was not godly. He also healed several people of serious illnesses and then claimed to be

God himself. What punishment would you give this criminal?

Explain that the last defendant is Jesus. The Sanhedrin or Jewish Council, and Pilate decided that death was a suitable punishment for his 'crimes'. Discuss whether this was a suitable punishment, and compare their thoughts. Tell them that in today's session, they are going to be looking at why Jesus died on the cross.

## THERE IS A REDEEMER
**Bible**
**For all groups**
**10 minutes**

Aim: to discover that, through his death, Jesus has redeemed us.

## WHAT YOU NEED
- Bibles

## WHAT YOU DO
This section takes the form of a talk and can be delivered exactly how it is written or you can adapt it to better suit your group.

Does anyone know what a 'Redeemer' is? Why do we need a Redeemer in our lives?

A Redeemer is someone who comes to save. Picture scenes from films like Harry Potter, Spider-Man, The Lord of the Rings. Every one of these films has a redemptive theme in them. When the situation gets so bad that there seems no escape, enter…

the Redeemer, Saviour – and everything is no longer quite so bad!

Jesus came to earth as a Redeemer – that was the point of him coming. Jesus was the solution in God's master plan to save the human race. God had tried everything else, so this was his last option.

In order to understand Jesus' mission to earth, listen to this illustration:
'A bus driver drove the school run every day of the week. Each day he would get into his bus and drive the windy roads until he reached the steep hill leading to the village. Struggling, he would slowly climb the hill in his bus and then would drive around from house to house, picking up all the children for school. Then he would carefully and very slowly drive down the hill to the school in the next village.

One day, the bus driver was on his school run. He drove carefully around the windy roads and then very slowly and carefully up the steep hill. He picked up all the children from their houses and began driving down the steep hill towards the school.

As he drove further down the hill, the bus began to go faster and faster and as he approached a corner he applied the brake to slow the bus down. Nothing happened. He tried again. Nothing happened. The brakes had failed. What was he going to do? He had a bus full of children and the brakes on the bus had failed. He was going faster and faster!

Suddenly, the driver remembered a field at the bottom of the hill. If he steered through the gate and into the field, he could drive around until the bus lost all its speed and stopped.

Ready to implement his plan, the driver aimed the speeding bus towards the gate to the field. Suddenly, the driver saw a little boy holding a ball standing in front of the gate that the driver was aiming for. The driver had to make a split-second decision – save one boy, or twenty children…?

As the bus came to a stop in the field, the emergency services tended to the twenty frightened, but safe children. The driver walked over to where a blanket lay over the ground. A ball lay close by. The driver sank slowly to his knees and covered his eyes as he wept so hard that his shoulders shook. He reached out and placed a hand on the body under the blanket and mourned the loss of his one and only son, whom he had sacrificed to save the lives of the other children on his bus.'

God was a bit like the bus driver. The only way for humanity to be saved from our descent into destruction was by God sending Jesus – his one and only Son – to live amongst us and to tell us of his love for us. Jesus then died on the cross to pay the price of our sin. He could have saved himself, but that was not God's will and he knew it. Jesus willingly died so that we might live and be free from all the wrong things we do.

The bus driver sacrificed his one and only son so that he could save all the other children on his bus from dying. God willingly sacrificed his one and only Son to save the whole of humanity from our sin.

The Bible says: 'This is how much God loved the world: He gave his Son, his one and only Son. And this is why: so that no one need be destroyed; by believing in him, anyone can have a whole and lasting life. God didn't go to all the trouble of sending his Son merely to point an accusing finger, telling the world how bad it was. He came to help, to put the world right again. Anyone who trusts in him is acquitted; anyone who refuses to trust him has long since been under the death sentence without knowing it. And why? Because of that person's failure to believe in the one-of-a-kind Son of God when introduced to him.' John 3:16–18 *(The Message)*

We all need Jesus, our personal Redeemer, to save us from all the bad things we do and say. Just as *Harry Potter*, *Spider-Man* and *The Lord of the Rings* all have redeemers, Jesus is ours.

You might want to break into smaller groups to discuss this. What is the young person's reaction to the story of the bus driver? And then what God did through the sacrifice of Jesus? You may want to look at Romans 5:1–11 together and explore a bit more what Jesus' death means. Be ready to tell your own story of what this means to you.

## MY PERSONAL REDEEMER
**Response**
**For all groups**
**5 minutes**

Aim: to encourage the group to think about what they have learned and how they can apply it to their lives.

## WHAT YOU DO
Ask the group to form pairs with someone that they really trust, and get them to sit together. Ask them to discuss the following things:
- What do you think about Jesus as your personal Redeemer?
- How do you feel about this?
- What are you going to do about it?

Invite them to pray for each other if they feel ready. If not, get them to spend some time reflecting upon what they have been discussing. You might want to have copies of *What Now?* (SU, £2.99, 9781844275397) as this will help the young people who might want to take a step forward in their spiritual journey.

# EVENT 4

## DRESSAGE / JESUS BRINGS FREEDOM

### TARGET

To discover that life with Jesus is not about being bound by rules that restrict us, but is about being set free by him!

### KEY PASSAGE

John 8:31,32; Matthew 7:24,25

### TRAINING FOR YOU

Think about your own life for a moment? How are you doing with following God's way? Take a look at Matthew 7:24–29. This passage tells us about the need to listen and obey Jesus' commands. Doing this gives us a solid foundation and frees us from worrying about whether the storms of life will drag us off track. But is that true of your own life at the moment? If knowing the truth sets you free (John 8:31,32), how well do you know the truth? How often do you read the Bible for yourself? Not to prepare a session, but personally, in order to get to know God (and his truth) better? Reflect on this now – how can you fit this into your daily life more?

### FOR YOUNG PEOPLE OUTSIDE A CHURCH COMMUNITY

Young people who have little or no previous experience of church may have the preconception that following Jesus means that they have to follow lots of rules, and that being a Christian means that they immediately have to become dull and boring! The concept that Jesus frees us from the wrong things that we do, rather than insisting that we follow a load of rules will be quite alien to young people.

### FOR CHURCH YOUNG PEOPLE

Many church young people will have the opinion that the Bible is merely a book of instructions and guidelines of how to live their life. And who reads the instruction manual? Yet the Bible is about God's love for us and his plan to bring us back to him. Yes, there are commands in there, guidelines on how to live with each other and with God, but these are more than an instruction manual. Challenge church young people about their relationship with God and how they view living his way for their whole lives.

**British Dressage**
www.britishdressage.co.uk
**British Equestrian Foundation**
www.bef.co.uk

# ASSEMBLY/ BASIC TALK OUTLINE

Aim: to discover that life with Jesus is not about being bound by rules that restrict us, but is about being set free by him!

## WHAT YOU NEED
• Music and sound system
• Horse tack (optional)

Before the session, ask a couple of volunteers to prepare a dressage routine. This involves two people adopting a 'wheelbarrow' posture, demonstrating some basic movements, eg walk, trot, turn 360 degrees, move diagonally, and a few comedy moves of their own creation.

Introduce the idea of horse riding and 'dressage' to the group, sometimes described as 'horse ballet'. Start the music, and let the team perform its routine, drawing attention to the moves. Invite some pairs of volunteers from the audience to attempt the routine. Either perform it there and then, or if there is room, let them rehearse with the team to perform it after the message. Award points for balance, rhythm, suppleness and obedience of the horse, and its harmony with the rider.

In horse riding, horses need to be trained and the rider uses their body, the reins, bridle and bit, to encourage the horse to move where they want it to go. This is how the rider in dressage trains the horse to work in this graceful way. (Show any tack that you have brought with you, explaining what it is.)

Ask: 'Is the horse free to go where it wants?' Well, no it isn't. Although the rider isn't physically forcing the horse to do what the rider wants, the training and the actions of the rider encourage the horse to act in a certain way and go in a certain direction. Ask: 'Are we free to do what we want?' (Get some feedback from the group about why they can't do what they want all the time.) Then talk about things we do that we know are wrong, but can't stop ourselves from doing. Is anyone forcing us to do that stuff? No, but the desires of our own heart and the habits we have formed lead us down that path again and again.

Can we be free from that stuff? Read John 8:31,32. Explain that some people think being a Christian is all about following rules, and that all Jesus wants to do is to stop us having fun. But Christians believe it's actually the opposite. Jesus is promising to set people free: free from those wrong things we do, but can't stop ourselves from doing. (You may like to refer back to ideas found in the previous section.)

Ask the group to think about something they do that they would like to stop. What would it be like if they could be set free from that? Leave a moment of quiet for the group to reflect.

# RESOURCES FOR 11 TO 14S

## TO OBEY OR NOT?

**Introductory activity**
**For all groups**
**10 minutes**

Aim: to help young people understand that we face the challenge of obedience in all aspects of our lives – yet obedience is not easy for many different reasons.

### WHAT YOU NEED

- Video clips of horses running free and horses being trained (optional, available to view on sites such as YouTube)
- A laptop and projector (optional)
- Paper and pens

### WHAT YOU DO

If you're using them, show the clips you have found of free and trained horses. Ask the young people to think about words that describe the free horses and those being trained. Who are they obeying?

Go on to ask the young people to list out the different types of people that they might be expected to obey. Hopefully, they will list out the following types of people:

- parents
- teachers
- police
- God

Once you have the list, write the words on separate sheets of paper and position each sheet at a different part of the room.

Ask the young people to go to the paper that has the type of person that they find easiest to obey. Take a moment to ask them why this is the case.

Now ask the young people to go to the paper that has the type of person that they find more difficult to obey. Again, ask them why this is the case.

Get the group back together and ask them the following questions:

- Why do we find being obedient so difficult?
- Are we free to choose who we obey?
- Why should we do what God wants?
- Why would we not do what God wants?

## THE DECISION IS YOURS…

**Introductory activity**
**For all groups**
**10 minutes**

Aim: to show that, unlike remote-controlled cars or scalextric cars, we all have free will.

### WHAT YOU NEED

- Two or three remote-controlled cars or a Scalextric set
- Medal or victory wreath (optional)

### WHAT YOU DO

Set the room up with a track and have the remote-controlled cars/Scalextric on the grid ready to set off. Ask the group to nominate their favourite car and ask them to give the reason why their choice is the best (nice colour, looks fast, go-faster

stripe). Allow the cars three complete circuits of the room and present the winner with a medal (second and third too).

Now ask the group to sit and ask the following questions:

- What is the difference between these cars and us?
- Thinking back to dressage, what differences are there between horses, us and these cars?
- What were these cars designed to do?
- What are we designed to do?

Explain that we are designed to have free will. Explain that God really took a chance on us by giving us free will. We can choose to be obedient or disobedient.

## WHY OBEY?

**Bible**
**For all groups**
**10 minutes**

Aim: to help the group understand that our love for Jesus is shown by our obedience to him – obedience comes out of love.

### WHAT YOU NEED

• Bibles

### WHAT YOU DO

Put the young people into small groups and ask each group to read the story of the wise and foolish builders (Matthew 7:24,25). Each group has to create a short role play to tell this story. They can modernise the story but the key point has to come across.

Once you've enjoyed each of the performances, ask the group what they believe was the main point that Jesus was making from this story: hearing Jesus' words and acting on them gives us the best foundation for our lives.

Now ask the following questions:
• Why should we be obedient to God?
• Why might we find it so hard to be obedient to God?

In the discussion, especially if you have young people from outside a church community in your group, you might want to explore the idea that most of the time people don't follow God because they think he is a spoilsport. It would be good to have one of the leaders tell a story from their life, where following God's ways has released them from stuff that was holding them back. It might be gossip that was threatening to destroy a friendship, or following God's way at work. An authentic story of the firm foundation of following God's way will speak loudly to young people from both within and outside your church community. Try to draw out from the story that obedience comes not from being forced to, but out of love for God.

Jesus was once asked: 'What is the greatest commandment?' Read Jesus' answer together from Mark 12:30,31. In essence, Jesus was saying that the greatest commandment was that we 'love God and each other'.

Ask the group:
• How would Jesus know that we love him?
• What does this mean in practice?

Our obedience comes, not because God makes us obey, but because we love God and want to do what makes him happy! What does this say about any freedom that Jesus brings?

## CHOOSE TO OBEY

**Response**
**For all groups**
**10 minutes**

Aim: to encourage the young people to reflect on being obedient to God.

### WHAT YOU NEED

• Horse-shaped pieces of paper or an outline of a horse on a large sheet of paper
• Felt-tip pens
• Envelopes (optional)

### WHAT YOU DO

Invite the young people to write down one or more areas of their lives where they feel they need to be more obedient to God. You could do this individually, or together on one large sheet of paper if your group is an established one.

Once they have done this, you could do any one of the following options:
• encourage them to close their eyes and pray in silence that God will help them in this area.
• invite them to share their thoughts, if not too personal, in a small group and pray for each other.
• ask them to write a prayer asking God for help in this area, and to keep it with them for the following week.
• put their paper horse in an envelope and post it to them in a couple of weeks to remind them what they committed to.

Talk again about the fact that obedience to God doesn't mean slavery, but freedom!

# RESOURCES FOR 14 TO 18S

## FALL BACK
**Introductory activity**
**For all groups**
**5 minutes**

Aim: to explore the relationship between love, trust and obedience.

### WHAT YOU NEED
• Willing volunteers!

### WHAT YOU DO
Tell your group that you are going to try some 'trust exercises'. You can use one of the following exercises or some of your own (ensure health and safety at all times):

*Catch me if you can*
In pairs of similar size, one becomes a Faller and one the Catcher. The Faller should stand with their back towards their partner and allow themselves to fall backwards. The Catcher should catch them! (You may want to be the Catcher yourself or run this game on a crash mat!)

*Lean on me*
Organise your young people into groups of about eight. Have them stand in a circle with one person in the middle. That person should close their eyes and lean into the arms of the circle. They can then be passed around the group.

Discuss with the group:
• What did the volunteers have to do to feel safe?
• Would you have taken part in this exercise if you didn't trust others?

• What might have happened if the volunteer had not properly obeyed the instructions?
• Is it easy to obey people you don't trust?

If we love someone, we trust them. If we trust them we're more likely to obey them.

## A NEW HOPE
**Introductory activity**
**For all groups**
**10 minutes**

Aim: to think more about the theme of freedom and obedience

### WHAT YOU NEED
• *Star Wars: A New Hope* on DVD
• A DVD player and TV or laptop and projector

### WHAT YOU DO
Play the clip from the film *Star Wars: A New Hope*. (Start clip at 00:40:48 and end at 00:43:00.)
Luke Skywalker and Obi Wan Kenobi have travelled to Mos Eisley to meet up with Han Solo. They get stopped by some StormTroopers looking for C3PO and R2D2, the droids that are with Luke and Obi Wan. Obi Wan uses 'The Force' to make the StormTroopers obey him.

Use the clip to start some discussion:
• What are the similarities between the way horses are controlled in dressage and Obi Wan's control in the clip?

• Does anyone in the group like the idea of having some sort of supernatural power that will allow them to make people obey them?
• What would you make people do?
• What outside forces in the world can influence the way they act?
• Why doesn't God use something like 'The Force' to make us obey him?

## HOUSE OF CARDS
**Bible**
**For all groups**
**10 minutes**

Aim: to explore how listening to Jesus and obeying gives a strong foundation for life, and brings us freedom.

### WHAT YOU NEED
• Packs of cards
• Bibles

### WHAT YOU DO
Either as one group, or in pairs and threes, challenge the young people to build a house of playing cards. After a while see who has built the highest house, then ask them how easy it was to do. What is needed to build a good house? This should bring out a few ideas, but make sure that they mention having a firm foundation, a stable flat surface.

Read Matthew 7:24–29 and decide together what the firm foundation being talked about here is. What's the group's reaction to this story? Do they agree with

Jesus' teaching here? It would be good to have one of your leaders tell a story from their life when listening to Jesus and obeying him has meant that they weren't worried when circumstances changed or when their life became more difficult. Authentic stories from your life will speak strongly of the power of loving God and living his way.

Get the young people to ask questions of this leader (make sure before the session that the leader is happy to be questioned!) about their story.

## OVER THE CLIFF?
**Bible**
**For church groups**
**15 minutes**

Aim: to explore the freedom that Jesus can bring.

### WHAT YOU NEED
• A large sheet of paper and marker pens
• Bibles
• A laptop and Internet access

### WHAT YOU DO
Brainstorm some of the things that can trap people in their daily lives and write them down on the sheet of paper. You might come up with things like drugs and alcohol, poverty, depression, or illness. Chat about how difficult it is to free yourself from situations like these.

Give out the Bibles and read Luke 8:26–39 together. Get the group's immediate reaction to the story: what surprises them? What confuses them? What makes them interested in the story?

Chat for a couple of minutes about what is the man trapped by and how Jesus frees him. Then go on to think about the reaction of the man compared to the reactions of the people who are watching. What does the man go on to do once he has been set free?

Does the group think that Jesus can create this kind of freedom today? Look back at the list you created at the start of this activity. Go on to the *I Am Second* website (**www.iamsecond.com**) and select some of the testimonies that are most appropriate to your group, and watch together how Jesus has freed people from difficult situations.

Go on to consider the question:
• Where does obedience fit in to this freedom?

Think about how the man obeyed Jesus at the end of the Bible passage. How did some of the people in the testimonies obey Jesus?

## GET INTO THE WORD
**Response**
**For all groups**
**5 minutes**

Aim: to discover more about God by getting to know him better through his Word.

### WHAT YOU DO
Explain to the group that one way we can learn more about the freedom God offers is to get to know him better. This is so that they know what he wants them to do, and also because they don't obey people unless they love and trust them first.

The greatest way we can get to know God better and to understand what he wants for our lives is to read the Bible. If we read what someone's written we get to know what they're into, what they're passionate about.

Challenge the group to all commit to reading the Bible more. This doesn't have to be every day, maybe just a couple of times a week to start with. It's got to be something they can achieve. You can increase the frequency later! Make a plan, to all read the same Bible passages, then in your next meeting, you can catch up with how everyone has got on.

From Scripture Union, go to **www.wordlive.org** or search for E100Y at **www.scriptureunion.org.uk**.

From YFC, get hold of YPs or *Mettle* from **www.yfc.co.uk**.

# EVENT 5

## SHOT PUT / WHO SETS YOUR DIRECTION?

### TARGET

To explore that following God means we need to choose the right path.

### KEY PASSAGE

Matthew 4:17–22

### TRAINING FOR YOU

Whether you've been a Christian for a long time or a few months, reading about the readiness with which Peter, Andrew, James and John drop their fishing business to follow Jesus, is incredibly disarming. In the equivalent passage in Luke (5:1–11), Jesus performs a miracle with their catch which must convince them that there is something different about him. But here, all Jesus does is call them: 'Follow me.' What would your response have been? When Jesus called you, what was your response? Was it immediate? Or did it take a long time to be convinced to follow? Young people face a lot of calls in their lives and you may be introducing them to Jesus' call for the first time today. But as you play your chosen games and activities, how can you talk about the time when Jesus called you, and the trajectory on which your life is travelling?

### FOR YOUNG PEOPLE OUTSIDE A CHURCH COMMUNITY

The actions of the fishermen are going to be surprising for those outside a church community. What evidence did these men have to drop everything and follow Jesus? The fact their lives changed completely when they changed paths to be with Jesus might be alarming to some. They may be comfortable with their lives, and with how the world directs their path. But Jesus' call is radical. Be ready to share your own story and be (appropriately) honest about how your path has been so far.

### FOR CHURCH YOUNG PEOPLE

You may have young people from a church group who are happy living a double life – 'Christian' at church, but following their own way for the rest of the time. The call of Jesus to follow his path – to change the trajectory of their lives – may be uncomfortable. What might they have to change about their lives?

UK Athletics
www.uka.org.uk

# ASSEMBLY/ BASIC TALK OUTLINE

Aim: to explore that following God means we need to choose the right path.

## WHAT YOU NEED
- Beanbags
- A large plastic hula hoop or masking tape
- A long tape measure
- A pen/pencil and paper (for scoring)

## WHAT YOU DO
Place the hula hoop at one end of your space and ask for a few volunteers. These competitors must stand in the hula hoop and throw the beanbag by making a pushing motion from their shoulder with the beanbag supported in the palm of their hand. They can spin around in the area designated by the hula hoop prior to throwing, but must not step out of it, otherwise they will be disqualified. (If you have no hula hoop, mark a line on the floor using masking tape.) Give each competitor three throws.

Measure the distance each competitor throws the beanbag shot put and award a small prize for the person who wins, and another for the person who tried hardest.

There are two things you need to get right if you are going to win the shot put. The first is the angle of projection. Experts suggest that there is a perfect angle you need to aim for, which is 40 degrees. More than this, you will send it too high and not get the distance. Lower than this, and you won't get the height needed to send it a long way. Then, when you have the angle sussed, you need to put as much of your weight behind the throw as you can. This is how you win.

Just as the angle of projection will determine where the shot put goes, in our lives, it's our beliefs and values that determine where we will end up. Most of us would agree that we want to end up in the same place – living a happy and fulfilled life. But have we set our direction right? Some people believe that the best way of getting there is by getting as much money and stuff as they can. Some people believe it's by having the perfect face or body. Some people think it's by having as many people as possible love and adore them. However, it seems that often, even when people have all of these things, they are still not happy or satisfied. So what's gone wrong?

The Bible teaches that God's way of doing life is the only one that is going to get us where we want to go. It says in the Psalms that God 'has shown us the path that leads to life' (Psalm 16:11). Living with our eyes and ears open to what God wants us to do and where he wants us to go is the only way we really find the full and happy life we're looking for. That usually means learning to obey his teachings about how we act towards other people, and what we do with our time, energy and possessions. And when we have seen what he is asking us to do, we need to do it with everything we've got!

# RESOURCES FOR 11 TO 14S

## DECISION TREE

**Introductory activity**
**For all groups**
**5 minutes**

### WHAT YOU NEED

- copies of the decision tree from page 74

### WHAT YOU DO

Give out copies of the decision tree and ask the young people to go through it. They could do this on their own, or in pairs or threes. When everyone has finished, ask for some feedback. What do they think of where their decisions took them? Do they think the destination they ended up in was a fair reflection of the decisions they'd taken?

Talk for a few moments about the decisions that the young people take in their every day lives. What are the most important decisions? Which ones seem inconsequential, but actually make a big difference? Go on to chat about how people make decisions – what people or things have an influence on the young people?

## FOLLOW ME

**Bible**
**For all groups**
**20 minutes**

Aim: to examine how the disciples responded to the call of God to 'follow', and how we may be called to follow him.

### WHAT YOU NEED

- Bibles

### WHAT YOU DO

Sit your group in a circle. Explain that you are going to read out a number of scenarios and that you would like volunteers to go into the middle of the circle to act out how they might react in the given situation. You could have more than one actor for each scenario.

Read out the following scenarios, and encourage your actors to react!
- Your mum asks you to tidy up your bedroom.
- Your teacher tells you to tuck in your shirt and put on your tie.
- A park keeper shouts at you to keep off the grass.
- Your teammate wants you to pass the ball to him.
- A radio competition says that if you get down to your local supermarket and meet the presenter, you could win £10,000!
- Your flight number is called for a summer holiday in the sun.

As the young people role-play these scenarios, ask them why they would react in the way they chose. Would other people react differently? Would they react immediately? Why do they react differently to some types of situations than to others?

Hand out Bibles and read Matthew 4:17–22. Discuss these questions:
- How did the disciples react when Jesus called them to 'follow me'?
- Why do you think they responded immediately?
- What sacrifices did they make?
- Why do you think they were prepared to drop everything?

End by discussing situations in which God might ask us to follow him, eg in our lifestyles, in the choices we make about our future, in our characters. What might prevent us from following him and what might help us?

# I WILL FOLLOW

**Bible**
**For church groups**
**10 minutes**

Aim: to reflect on what made the young people follow God and to check on their lives' trajectories.

## WHAT YOU NEED

- Bibles
- Concordances, study Bibles and Bible encyclopedias
- Reflective music and the means to play it

## WHAT YOU DO

Gather the young people together and explain that you are all going to reflect on why you follow Jesus. Read Matthew 4:17–22 out to the group and then ask them to settle down somewhere comfortable. Play the music and lead the group through these questions (leave space for the young people to think about their answers before moving on to the next question):

- When was the first time that Jesus called you to follow him?
- What was your reaction? Did you drop everything like Peter, Andrew, James and John? Or were you more reluctant?
- How long have you been following Jesus? Have you changed or grown during that time? How different are you from the person that Jesus first called?
- Are you still following Jesus? What's the trajectory of your life like?

Stop the music and share around the reference books you have brought with you. Ask the group to look for references to Peter, Andrew, James and John. How did they change after being called? What was the trajectory of their lives like? (This will be easier for Peter than the others!)

Get back together and share any feedback. What can the group learn from these disciples?

# SHOT-PUT PRAYERS

**Response**
**For all groups**
**10 minutes**

Aim: to encourage your group to pray for each other that they will be able to follow God in their lives.

## WHAT YOU NEED

- An outline of a shot-putter
- Circles of paper
- Blu-tack
- Pens
- Masking tape

## WHAT YOU DO

Stick the outline of the shot-putter to the wall and mark a line with masking tape going up 40 degrees from the shot-putter (the perfect trajectory for the shot).

Hand out a circle of paper and pen to each young person. Explain that you want them to think of a situation in which they want to follow God. It may be that they want to start following him for the first time; maybe they have an area of their lifestyle that they want to get going in God's direction; or perhaps they have decisions to make about their future.

Encourage them to write these situations down on their circle – in as much or as little detail as they feel comfortable with. Ask them to think about how well they are doing in that situation. If they're doing well and would like God's help to carry on, then they should stick their circle close to the line of perfect trajectory. If they're doing badly in a situation, they should place their circle further away from the perfect line. This activity requires a certain amount of trust which some of your group may not yet have, so don't put pressure on any young people to stick their circle on the wall. Let them keep their circles if the want to.

End by asking the group to read each other's circles. Ask the young people to pray about the things written on them – they may simply like to ask God to help the writer to follow him.

# RESOURCES FOR 14 TO 18S

## MAKE THE CHOICE

**Introductory activity**
**For all groups**
**15 minutes**

Aim: to help young people understand that following God is a choice we can all make.

### WHAT YOU NEED

- *The Matrix* on DVD
- A DVD player and TV or laptop and projector
- Paper and pens (optional)

### WHAT YOU DO

*The Matrix* tells the story of Neo (Keanu Reeves), a blank-faced computer whizz who's about to go through the looking glass – out of the late 20th-century world as he knows it, into the real, post-apocalyptic 'desert of the real'.

It's where robots rule the planet and keep humans plugged into a virtual reality matrix, living in a dream world while their energy fuels the machines.

Play the clip from *The Matrix* (from 00:25:10 to 00:29:50) in which Neo has a choice to make – he is offered two pills. The blue one will allow him to live a 'normal' life, forgetting all he has learned about the Matrix; the red pill will enable him to see the difficult truths of the Matrix. Neo chooses the red pill.

*The Matrix* is certificate 15, so be aware if there are any 14-year-olds in your group.

Discuss the following points:
- What choice did Neo face and why do you think he chose the red pill?
- Do you think it was an easy choice? Do you think he made the right choice?
- What difficult choices have you faced?
- How did you make those choices?

Think about the trajectory of Neo's life. If you like, using paper and pens, map out the two paths of Neo's life – one for if he had not taken the pill, and one for when he did. How would they have been different? Then think about a decision you have faced – how different would the trajectory of your life been if you had made a different decision? (This point could also be illustrated by 'Turn Left', episode 11 of *Doctor Who*, series 4, where Donna is persuaded to make a different decision and a whole alternate universe is formed.)

## MAP READING

**Introductory activity**
**For all groups**
**10 minutes**

Aim: to think about the methods we use to find our way to unknown destinations.

### WHAT YOU NEED

- Two copies of a street map showing the area around your building

### WHAT YOU DO

Before the session, choose two different locations in your local area that are the same distance from your building. Mark these on the maps, one on each copy. The distance from your church will depend on how long you want the activity to last. Station a leader at each of these locations, and all leaders should synchronise their watches to ensure fairness.

Divide your group into two teams (with a couple of leaders in each one) and give each of them a map with their end location marked on it. At least one person in each group should have a mobile phone with your number programmed into it. At your signal they must race to reach the location marked on their map by whatever they judge to be the fastest route. Groups must stay together or be disqualified.

When they arrive at their end location the leader notes the time of arrival and escorts them back to the starting point to find out who won. You may choose to give a prize to the winning team.

Once everyone is back, discuss briefly whether this activity would have been possible without the maps. What other methods could your groups have used for finding their way to an unknown destination?

Discuss how the group makes decisions in their life? What trajectory is their life on at the moment?

Note: make sure you have permission from parents/guardians to take young people off-site (there are sample forms on page 76). Risk assess this activity and brief the young people carefully before you start (see page 78).

## ASK, SEEK, KNOCK
**Bible**
**For all groups**
**20 minutes**

Aim: to explore the fact that God promises to guide us in our lives.

### WHAT YOU NEED
• Copies of page 75
• A set of Christian magnetic poetry (available from larger bookshops or online, though you could use other magnetic poetry)
• A large metal notice board or surface
• A large map (area covered is not important)
• A pin board large enough to display the map on
• Blue and red map pins
• Paper and pens
• Envelopes
• Bibles

Before the session, set up three separate tables in different parts of the room.

On the first table, place the metal notice board and the magnetic poetry, and copies of the sheet 'ASK'. On the second table, place the pin board with the map fixed to it and the map pins, and copies of the sheet 'SEEK'. On the third, place paper, pens and envelopes, and copies of the sheet 'KNOCK'.

If we decide to try and follow God, one of the first questions we have to ask is: 'What does God want me to do?' How do we know what God wants us to do? This can seem very confusing. Jesus said something that can help us with this.

Read Matthew 7:7–12 together and then explain that you have set up three stations around the room to help the group explore this passage further. Everyone should go at their own pace and try each activity out.

Allow five to ten minutes for people to explore and participate in the activities. When everyone has finished, read the passage aloud again to close. If appropriate, provide an opportunity for your group to give their reflections on what they have learned and experienced.

## LIFE MAPS
**Response**
**For all groups**
**20 minutes**

Aim: to reflect on our personal journeys with God, and to think about our 'trajectory'.

### WHAT YOU NEED
• Paper and art materials (paints, coloured pens or pencils, pastels etc)

### WHAT YOU DO
Explain to the group that this activity is a way to help us think about our own journey with God. We are each going to create a picture which represents our life and the milestones we have covered. Think about how you would like to portray the difficult times and the good. How will you show where God is present and where you felt alone? Can you see the pathway ahead or is it more of a maze?

Explain to the group that their picture can be an abstract pattern or a figurative representation – there will be no artistic criticism of their efforts!

Allow up to 15 minutes for people to complete their pictures. If they are willing, encourage some of them to talk about what they have drawn and why. To close, say a short prayer over the pictures, asking God to bless each of our journeys with him.

# EVENT 6
## MODERN PENTATHLON/GOD'S GIFTS

### TARGET
To discover that God has given us all different talents, and that when we work together, we achieve more.

### KEY PASSAGE
1 Corinthians 12

### TRAINING FOR YOU
Young people can be so confusing! One moment they can insist that they're the best at something, showing you their talent at skateboarding/dancing/crochet, and then the next, say that they're not good at anything. Our insecurities can often mirror those in our group. It's easy to think that others are better at speaking, organisation or talking with young people. It's easy to get overawed by others who seem more experienced, gifted or 'called' to youth work. However, you're working with young people because God has called you and has given you the gifts and skills to do it. We may not have *all* the skills to run the perfect youth ministry, but that's what a team is for! Read 1 Corinthians 12 and reflect on what gifts God has given you. Are you using them wisely and well, or are you trying to do things you're not all that gifted at? Talk to God about how you see your gifts and skills. Be honest with him.

### FOR YOUNG PEOPLE OUTSIDE A CHURCH COMMUNITY
Depending on their background, young people from outside your community might struggle to see what they are good at. The idea that God has given them gifts and skills may be surprising to them. Be ready to sensitively discuss with these young people what their gifts might be – God could bring a complete new revelation and change young people's lives this session!

### FOR CHURCH YOUNG PEOPLE
Church young people may have discussed different gifts before, but never really thought how they can use them. Challenge these young people to see how their gifts can be used now for God, both in your church and in the wider community.

**Pentathlon GB**
www.pentathlongb.org

# ASSEMBLY/ BASIC TALK OUTLINE

Aim: to discover that God has given us all different talents, and that when we work together, we achieve more.

## WHAT YOU NEED

- Some kind of shooting range, eg hoops with beanbags, tin cans and balls, or even a 'teacher in the stocks' event
- A running route of an appropriate size – this could be on a designated track or simply around your space

## WHAT YOU DO

Select some competitors. Each one must run the pre-set route once round. When they approach the shooting range, they must hit the target three times (they may have unlimited shots). Repeat this process three times (or however many times is appropriate for the length of time you have for the session). On the last time round the track, the young people should head for the finish line. The winner is simply the first person to cross it.

You may like to vary the event with each round, for example by amending the difficulty levels of the shooting challenge each time (smaller target, greater distance), making the young people run backwards for a lap, putting some small hurdles in place for a lap etc.

One of the most incredible events in the Olympics is the modern pentathlon. We can easily admire athletes for being able to run fast, or swimmers for being able to swim hard and fast, or equestrians for their skill with horses. But imagine being so skilled as to be able to do all of these well – not to mention shooting and fencing?! Five tough events, and all the competitors seem to take it in their stride!

If somebody asked you what you were skilled at, what would you say? You might immediately think of a sport you enjoy and say you were good at that. You might think of your ability to play an instrument. You may not be able to think of anything, and you might say that you don't have any skills or talents. This is simply not true. The Bible teaches that God has made each one of us and given us all different gifts that are unique to us. This doesn't mean that he has given some people a PS3 and others a Wii. 'Gifts' means things which are special to us, that we can use in our lives. Some people are good leaders: people who listen to what others have to say and respect it. Some people are good at looking out for people: they can notice when people are upset or in trouble. Some people are good teachers: they can help people understand important things, or see things from a different point of view.

If you look carefully at yourself, you will see that you have a gift – probably lots! So ask yourself, what is it, and what should I be doing with it? The Bible says that when we offer what we have to God, he can use it in ways we could never imagine – in life- and world-changing ways. Now that is incredible!

45

# RESOURCES FOR 11 TO 14S

## PARTY TRICKS

**Introductory activity**
**For all groups**
**10 minutes**

Aim: to start thinking about all having different skills and talents

### WHAT YOU DO

Ask your group if any of them have any party tricks, eg impressions, juggling, magic, doing strange things with their bodies! It may be a good idea to prime them the week before the meeting.

Spend some time talking about and watching each other's party tricks. Have a 'Clap-o-meter' vote for your group's favourite party trick.

See if anyone can do five separate tricks, for example, a cartwheel, a magic trick, play the recorder with their nose, sing the national anthem and then speak fluent Romanian! This will be much more challenging! Talk about the talents that people who compete in multi-events, such as the modern pentathlon, must have. Chat about the difficulties and challenges this must bring.

## GIFTS AND TALENTS AUDIT

**Introductory activity**
**For all groups**
**10 minutes**

Aim: to help young people consider their own gifts in the context of school.

### WHAT YOU DO

Gather the group together and discuss the following points. If you have a large number of young people, you may want to divide up into smaller groups.

- In what areas do you feel 'strong' at school?
- In what areas do you feel 'weak'?
- How would you describe your gifts and talents?

Encourage your group to think wider than just 'subjects', eg are they a strong friend, a conscientious pupil, involved in any clubs? Explain to the young people that we often have to work and do things in areas that we do not feel strong (particularly at school). For example, some of us might have to work hard at maths whilst others struggle in PE. However, we all have gifts and talents that can be developed at school.

## BODY BUILDING

**Bible**
**For all groups**
**20 minutes**

Aim: to help young people understand that we all have different gifts and talents, and that they are all necessary and important.

### WHAT YOU NEED

- Bibles
- Pieces of mirrored card
- Pens

### WHAT YOU DO

Begin by asking each member of the group to state one gift or talent that they have at school. This could be subject based (eg 'I am good at English'), or it could be to do with the wider school community (eg 'I run a club' or 'I am a really good friend'). Draw attention to the wide range of strengths and talents in your group.

Hand out Bibles and read 1 Corinthians 12:4–6,12–20,27–31. (You may also like to read Romans 12:4–8 for a fuller list of gifts.) Get an immediate reaction from the group about the fact that our gifts and skills are given to us by God. How does that make them feel? Special because God has given *them* something? Embarrassed because they haven't used the gift as they should have? You may get a variety of reactions here.

Explain to the group that God has made us with a variety of gifts and talents; this variety enables us to work well together and to help each other (it wouldn't be much good if we could all play football but none of us could cook, for example).

Tell the group that you want them to consider the gifts and talents represented in their group. Give everyone a piece of mirrored card and ask them to write their name on the non-mirrored side at the top. Place the pieces of card around the room and ask the group to move round the room and write down on each person's card one thing that they are good at (eg being generous, encouraging, organising, creative). Keep the group moving and make sure that each card has comments written on. When everyone is finished, give the group time to find their card and read the positive comments.

End by taking feedback from the group and discussing the following points:

• What types of gifts are represented by your group?
• How could you help your friends in the group to make the most of their strengths and talents?
• How could you and your group use your strengths and talents to help others?
• Which of the gifts, listed in the Romans and 1 Corinthians passages, do you recognise within your group?
• And which gifts have you suddenly discovered you've got? What are you going to do about that?!

## USE YOUR GIFTS!

**Bible**
**For church groups**
**10 minutes**

Aim: to explore the gifts we have and see how we can use them in our church communities.

### WHAT YOU NEED

• Bibles
• Paper and pens

### WHAT YOU DO

Before the session, you will need to talk to the leadership of your church to see where your young people can join in the ministry of the church family. This could be welcoming people, playing in the worship band, helping out with children's work, making tea and coffee – wherever people need help. You might also explore the possibility that the young people could start a new ministry.

With the group, explain that you are going to read 1 Corinthians 12:1–11 out, and that you want the young people to write down all the gifts and talents that they hear in the passage. When you have finished, share all the things the group has found.

It's likely that your church group will know each other quite well, so have a time where each person, on their own, thinks about the talents and gifts that the others in their group have. Make sure they understand that this is a serious exercise, and that they shouldn't write anything negative down, even as a joke!

Review together what people have said about each other. Make sure you have something about each person, in case anyone is left out. Then work together to see where people in your group might use these talents as part of the church family. Don't force people into doing something they don't want to, but be encouraging! Pray together about these things, then go out and make them happen!

## BUILD UP YOUR STRENGTH

**Response**
**For all groups**
**10 minutes**

Aim: to encourage young people to develop and use their God-given strengths and talents.

### WHAT YOU NEED

• Post-it® notes
• Pens
• Bibles

### WHAT YOU DO

Read Colossians 3:23,24. Explain to your group that God wants them to develop and use the gifts and talents he has given them. Remind them that this requires some effort on their part!

Hand out Post-it® notes and pens. Ask each young person to spend a few moments thinking of something they could do over the following week that could help them develop and/or use their gifts: eg practise their talent, ask a teacher to help them with something, commit to finishing their coursework, write a card to a friend.

Ask them to share their idea with someone else, who will check up on them the next time your group meets! Pray that your young people will use their gifts and talents to bring glory to their Creator over the coming week.

# RESOURCES FOR 14 TO 18S

## SING OUT LOUD

**Introductory activity**
**For all groups**
**20 minutes**

Aim: to introduce the theme of strengths and talents using discussion based on a current TV series.

### WHAT YOU NEED

- Clips of people auditioning for a talent show (see YouTube or other sites)
- Internet access and a laptop

### WHAT YOU DO

Show the clips of people auditioning for various talent shows. Make sure you've got a selection of good and bad. You might also want to include some things such as gymnastics and dance, to get away from just singing.

Get the young people's opinions about the competitors' talents (or lack of them). Does the fact that some of them can't sing (or dance) mean that they haven't got any talent at all?

Discuss the following questions with the group:

- Is a talent show environment a good way to discover whether you have a gift or not?
- What's helpful about it?
- What's unhelpful?
- Who has helped you to see whether you have gifts or talents?
- If you're not sure about whether you have a gift or not, what kind of help do you want to find out more?

Explain that today the group will be looking at their gifts and talents, and that we all have God-given gifts. While we are not good at everything, everyone shines at something, whether it is talking or being quiet, being a good leader or a good follower, a thinker or a doer. God gives us gifts for us to use for his glory, not our own.

## GOD-GIVEN GIFTS

**Bible**
**For all groups**
**20 minutes**

Aim: to help the young people to realise that they all have gifts and talents and are able to do God's work here on earth.

### WHAT YOU NEED

- Bibles
- Pens
- Large sheets of paper or wallpaper
- Post-it® notes.

### WHAT YOU DO

Together as a group (or if you have lots of young people, split them down into smaller groups), think about the gifts and talents that are needed to compete in a multi-event sport, such as Modern Pentathlon. What kind of skills do you need to shoot, ride, fence, run and swim? Write down these skills on one of the large sheets of paper.

Gather the group together and give out the Bibles, pens and paper. As a group read Romans 12:6–8 and write down the different gifts that Paul talks about in his letter to the Romans. Compare the two lists – what are the differences? What are the similarities?

Go on to discuss the following in your group:

- What do they think about the passage and the gifts that are listed?
- Do they think that they possess any of the gifts listed here?
- What gifts do they think they have/ what are they good at?
- How can they develop this strength or talent?
- How can they use this strength/talent or gift to serve God?

Give out the Post-it® notes and pens and ask everyone to write down on their note what gift/strength/talent they believe they have. Then underneath, ask them to write down how they think they can use this to serve God.

Roll out the wallpaper and get a young person to lie on top of it so that you can draw around their outline. Now ask all the young people to stick their Post-it® note on the part of the outline that is relevant to their talent. For example, if they are good at helping people, get them to stick their note onto the arms or hand of the outline.

When everyone has done this, take some time to look at the various gifts that the group has and how they can all serve

God's purposes on earth in one way or another.

## AFFIRMATION STALLION

**Response**
**For all groups**
**20 minutes**

Aim: to provide an opportunity for young people to hear from their peers about what their strengths and talents might be.

### WHAT YOU NEED

• A4 or A5 paper
• Felt-tip pens (water-based only)
• Masking or gaffer tape

### WHAT YOU DO

Give everyone a pen and stick a sheet of paper onto each person's back with the tape. Invite everyone to circulate for ten minutes or so and to write on other people's backs what they think their strengths and talents are. Encourage each person to write something on each other person's back, even if they don't know that person very well. If someone else has already written what they had planned to write, then they should still write the same thing so that a picture of key strengths and talents can be built up. Get people to think broadly – this is not about sport or academic achievement. People can have strengths in the arts, in relationships, in communication, and so on.

After everyone has written on every other person's back, get people to take their sheets off and sit down to read and reflect on them. Get them to use some different coloured felt-tip pens. Invite them to circle in one colour all those things that they are surprised to see written on their back. Then circle in another colour strengths or talents that get mentioned more than once. Then circle in another colour what they see as their main strength or talent.

After a period of reflection, get people to discuss their response to the sheets. Find out what people were surprised by, and what they agree with. Encourage people to think about how they could develop these strengths and talents.

End with a time of prayer, giving people the opportunity to offer their strengths and talents to God and asking him to help them develop them.

## WHEEL OF TALENTS

**Response**
**For all groups**
**20 minutes**

Aim: to provide an opportunity for young people to offer their strengths and talents to God.

### WHAT YOU NEED

• Large plastic hoop
• Coloured paper streamers (10 cm longer than the width of the hoop) – the more different colours the better
• A stapler or some sticky tape

### WHAT YOU DO

This activity gets individuals to reflect on themselves rather than on their peers. It will work better in a group that doesn't know each other so well. This activity should also be done in an atmosphere of worship – you may like to have some music playing in the background to enable people to focus.

Invite people to take a few streamers of different colours. On each one, get them to write a strength or talent that they think they have. Then get them to think about other people in the group – what gifts and talents do they think their friends have? Encourage them not to just think of the obvious, but to consider where their friends have special qualities. They should write the names of these people and the gifts and talents they have on other streamers.

Then invite people one by one to attach their streamers to the hoop weaving their streamers in and out of other people's. People may be shy about talking about their own talents, so don't force them. Encourage people to affirm each other and see if there are any talents that are recognised by several people.

Finish by inviting people to pray for each other, that God will affirm these gifts and talents and to give new ones as necessary, and that people will be able to develop their gifts and talents further.

# EVENT 7
## FOUR-PERSON RELAY / SERVING OTHERS

### TARGET
To explore the idea that Jesus calls us to think about others first, rather than only thinking about ourselves and what we can achieve.

### KEY PASSAGE
John 13:1–17

### TRAINING FOR YOU
The story of Jesus washing the disciples' feet may be a familiar one – after all, if comes up quite a lot! However, read John 13:1–17 now, as if it were the first time you had heard the story. What do you make of it? Jesus here is the picture of humility, performing a task that was usually performed by a servant or a slave. Peter's reaction gives us a picture of the surprising, almost shocking nature of what Jesus was doing. Would you have reacted like Peter? Would you have let Jesus do this menial task for you? Reflect for a moment on what this might mean for you, both in your own spiritual life, and in your work with young people? How ready are you to 'be' Jesus to the young people in a similar situation?

### FOR YOUNG PEOPLE OUTSIDE A CHURCH COMMUNITY
The idea of working together and serving others goes against the culture of celebrity and trying to get the best deal for yourself, regardless of how it affects others. Jesus' call to serve others is radically counter-cultural and young people from outside a church community may never have considered this an option in living their lives. As you go through this session, gently challenge young people to see how their actions affect those around them.

### FOR CHURCH YOUNG PEOPLE
Young people from your church may be more aware of Christ's call to serve, but many still might not be in a place where they think about others before themselves. Provide opportunities for them to be more active in church, helping them to see how much they are helping others in what they are doing.

UK Athletics
www.uka.org.uk
ASA
www.swimming.org/asa

# ASSEMBLY/ BASIC TALK OUTLINE

Aim: to explore the idea that Jesus calls us to think about others first, rather than only thinking about ourselves and what we can achieve.

## WHAT YOU NEED
• Range of silly dressing-up clothes

## WHAT YOU DO
Using teams of four young people, run a relay race using laps of the assembly hall. Instead of a baton, students need to pass on the ridiculous dressing-up gear they've been wearing.

If you are running this in a lesson context, you may want to focus on the real discipline of the relay, including the skill of passing over the baton, and save the 'silly' relay version until the end of the lesson.

Athletics events are, generally speaking, very much solo efforts. You run alone to beat the others. You aim to throw further than others, jump higher or longer than others. The relay stands out in contrast to these other athletics contests. In the relay, athletes must still run as fast as they can. But their efforts aren't just so that they can win. It's so others can win, too.

In our lives, we can be led to believe that we are living for our own sakes. We do well at school for our personal benefit and earn money so that we can live comfortably. But are we really so separate from other people? Jesus' big message that he brought to the world was that of love. He taught people to love their neighbour as themselves, and taught them the golden rule that we should do to other people what we would want them to do to us. He taught that we should give to people in need, to share what we have without complaining or expecting to get anything in return, and to remember the people that other people forget about. For Jesus, being human means being connected to others – and doing as well as we can so that we can help others.

Christians believe that God has gifted us all in many different ways. We all have different talents – things we are naturally good at. As we saw before, these go beyond being able to play an instrument or being a gifted sportsperson. This might mean being good at listening to people or being able to help people make peace with each other. We have all been given time and energy that can be used in any number of ways. Some of us may even have money and lots of nice things! The question is, what will we use all of these for? We all have a choice between using them for our own glory – to make sure that we get the limelight – or bringing other people into the limelight. The choice is ours.

# RESOURCES FOR 11 TO 14S

## FAST FAME OR FIRST PLACE?

Introductory activity
For all groups
10 minutes

Aim: to introduce the idea of being a servant.

### WHAT YOU NEED

• Flip-chart paper
• Marker pens
• Stopwatch

### WHAT YOU DO

Get the group to sit around the flip-chart paper. Explain that you are going to call out a category of people, and the group has 30 seconds to shout out as many people as possible who fit into that category. You are going to write them down as they shout them out (you may want another person to help you write).

Call out some of these categories below: athletes, footballers, pop stars, film stars, celebrities, politicians and world leaders.

Count up how many people the young people have thought of in 30 seconds for each one.

Now call out another category – 'servants'. It is likely that there will be very few, if any, names called out.

Now time for one last category – 'people vital to the running of society'.

In this category you are looking for answers such as police officers, doctors and nurses, charity workers. Count up how many you got in this category – how many of them could also be classed as 'servants'?

Say that being a servant is very unlikely to get us fame or fortune. Jesus knows that serving is not always glamorous work but it is vital, not only to the running of society, but to the well-being of mankind. That is why he wants us to serve others – for free – to show them how much we, and he, love them.

## WHO CLEANS HEAVEN?

Bible
For all groups
10 minutes

Aim: to explore the example of servanthood set by Jesus.

### WHAT YOU NEED

• *Bruce Almighty* DVD
• A DVD player and TV or laptop and projector
• Bibles

### WHAT YOU DO

Show the clip from *Bruce Almighty* (from 24:30 to 28:05). There we see Bruce meet the cleaner, then go upstairs and bump into 'God' (Morgan Freeman) who is the same person! This really confuses Bruce, whose first reaction is to laugh and walk away, claiming that the whole thing is a joke.

At the end of the clip, ask the group, 'Why do you think it took Bruce by surprise that God was also the cleaner?' Have any of them ever seen a famous person doing a bit of housework, or their head teacher picking up litter?

In Matthew 20:28, Jesus, the King of the universe, says that he has 'not come to be served', but '… to serve'. Here he states that he is going to do things the wrong way round and upside-down!

Read John 13:1–17. Ask the group if Jesus' actions surprise them. If so, why? How would they expect Jesus to act?

Go on to discuss these questions:
• How does Peter react?
• Is Peter's reaction similar to Bruce's?
• What message do you think Jesus was trying to get across to Peter?

What picture of Jesus does this leave the young people with? How do they see him now? What does this say to them about the way we should be living?

## FOOT WASHING AND BEYOND

Bible
For church groups
20 minutes

Aim: to be inspired by Jesus' washing of the disciples' feet, and to follow his example.

## WHAT YOU NEED

- Large bowls (such as washing-up bowls) filled with warm water
- Soap
- Towels
- Bibles
- Paper and pens

## WHAT YOU DO

Ask the young people to get into pairs, then explain that they are going to follow Jesus' example and wash each other's feet. Provide each pair with a bowl, warm water, etc.

If anyone is very reluctant to do one of the roles then link them up with someone who is OK about either having their feet washed or washing feet. Some people do have strong feelings about feet – so try a bit of gentle encouragement and then respect their feelings. You could also suggest that they wash each other's hands.

Ask for feedback as to how it felt to do the foot washing and how it felt to be the recipient. Ask them to discuss in pairs if they think this is a Christian thing to do and why they have come to that conclusion. Share their answers together.

Read John 13:1–17 from *The Message* (if possible) to the group. Explain that Jesus is not just demonstrating how good he is at cleaning feet; he is also demonstrating that by putting our trust in him and allowing him full access to our hearts and souls, he can make us clean on the inside, too.

Look at verse 10. Ask the group what they think that means. What are the areas of our lives that we find hard to keep holy? How can we allow Jesus to 'wash' us clean?

If you have time, read together John 13:34,35. Ensure the group understands that Jesus said this just before he was crucified – and did the most loving thing imaginable for them.

---

# AUCTION OF TALENTS

**Response**
**For all groups**
**Up to 60 minutes**

Aim: to allow the young people to serve others in their community and show the love of Jesus in practical ways.

## WHAT YOU NEED

- Card
- Pens
- A hammer
- Chairs
- Background music
- Refreshments

## WHAT YOU DO

Depending on the size of your group, you may want to do this either as the second half of your meeting, or a whole session in itself.

Create invitations for the parents/ guardians of the young people, inviting them to come to an 'Auction of Talents'.

Here, they can bid for a young person to come and do some work for them.

This is a great way of raising money for the youth group, the church, the homeless or a charity of your choice. Make it clear where the proceeds are going. The adults do not generally mind if the money goes back into the youth club, or is given to a charity, and they all enjoy bidding for someone to do a chore for them! The only rule is that the minimum bid is £1 and parents/guardians may not bid for a relative! Before the auction, ask the young people to think of something that they could offer to do.

Run the auction, offering one young person at a time. Ask them to explain their offer and then begin the bidding. The highest bidder wins and the money is paid. The young person then commits to making their bargain good by the end of the week. It's probably wise to have an adult supervise this.

If you really wanted to 'go to town' with this, invite the whole church and maybe even members of the community – and offer to clean whole streets, paint subways, collect trolleys, dig a garden, clean graffiti off shop walls etc. Let your imagination run wild! You could invite the local press and use it as an opportunity to serve the community.

At the end of the evening get the young people to serve the adults with tea, coffee and biscuits.

# RESOURCES FOR 14 TO 18S

## A SELFLESS ACT?

**Introductory activity**
**For all groups**
**15 minutes**

Aim: to introduce the theme by asking what motivates people to do things for others.

### WHAT YOU NEED
• Gummy sweets

### WHAT YOU DO
Divide the young people into two groups. Give everybody in one group ten gummy sweets, but don't give the other group anything.

Explain that the young people with the sweets are free to do whatever they want with them, and that if the other group wants any then that's between them and the young people with the sweets.

Sit back for a few minutes and see what happens. Discuss the outcome with the group. Some questions you may want to ask are:
• Did anyone without sweets manage to get any?
• How willing were the group with sweets to part with them?
• How did the second group try to convince the first group to give them sweets?
• Did they try bargaining?
• Did anyone just say 'please'?

Thinking about the relay, how do the competitors work together? What would happen if they didn't?

Discuss the following:
• Have you ever given something for the benefit of someone else?
• Have you ever given something and known that some good would come to you in return?
• Is there such a thing as a completely selfless act?

## FOLLOW MY EXAMPLE

**Bible**
**For church groups**
**10 minutes**

Aim: to look at the example of Jesus who was willing to serve.

### WHAT YOU NEED
• Bibles
• Paper and pens

### WHAT YOU DO
Serving other people may not be a very attractive proposition. Usually we like to be important, to be special, to have other people serve us. But as Christians we can't escape the fact that we are called to serve. If we find this hard to swallow, we need only look at the example of Jesus. If he was prepared to serve, how much more should we?

Either all together or in smaller groups (or even pairs), ask the young people to write down their impression of Jesus. What words would they use to describe him? If they were telling someone about him, how would they do it. Give the groups a few minutes to write a word picture (or even draw an actual picture) of Jesus, then get some feedback.

Read John 13:1–17 together. What did Jesus decide to do? Remind the group that the disciples would be walking around in sandals in a very hot, dry, dusty country. Their feet would have been filthy! Point out that the job of washing the feet of guests was usually given to the lowest servant. It was a way of welcoming guests and making them feel at home. The disciples didn't have any servants when they met to eat this Passover meal, and maybe they were all sitting there wondering which one of them was going to do it. They would never have guessed that Jesus would be the one.

Ask the group these questions:
• Why do you think Peter didn't want Jesus to wash his feet? Why did he change his mind?
• What impact do you think this experience would have had on the disciples? Point out that they were far more likely to follow Jesus' example, having seen him do it, than if he had just said, 'I want you to serve each other!'
• Foot washing isn't a part of our culture – it doesn't happen nowadays. What is an equivalent – a task in our society that happens regularly, that we could do for each other?
• How good are you at serving others? What stops you? How can you follow Jesus' example?

Ask the young people to look again at their word pictures of Jesus. Do they want to change anything after having looked at the Bible passage?

## FREE TO SERVE

**Bible**
**For all groups**
**15 minutes**

Aim: to think about how freedom can lead to service.

### WHAT YOU NEED

• Bibles

### WHAT YOU DO

Ask the group to imagine that they had £10,000, a week off school, college or work, and the ability to go wherever they liked without their parents tagging along. In other words, lots of freedom! What would they do? Get them to share their ideas.

Read together Galatians 5:1,13–26. Discuss with the group:
• People usually think of freedom as being the ability to do exactly what you want to do, with no restrictions. Is this Paul's idea of freedom? What does he say that Christians should use their freedom to do? Why?
• What are some of the things that Paul says people who just follow their own desires get into? How could serving

other people keep you from falling into these traps? You could get the group to focus on just one or two of these.
• How easy do you find it to serve other people? Be honest! What are some of the things that stop you serving?
• Paul lists the fruit of the Spirit in verses 22 and 23. Which of these would you most need if you were to serve other people more?

## COMMUNITY SERVICE

**Response**
**For all groups**
**30 minutes (plus time to carry out your project)**

Aim: to help young people to think about how they can together serve others in the community.

### WHAT YOU NEED

• Paper and pens

### WHAT YOU DO

It's unfortunate that community service is a phrase used to describe a type of punishment for a crime! But this type of community service shouldn't be done out of duty or reluctantly – it's supposed to be a choice to bless others. Doing something as part of a group can be a great learning experience as well as helping others.

You may want to team up with a project like 'The Noise' run by Soul Survivor. See their website for more details: **www.soulaction.org/soulsurvivor/index**

Another website you could look at is **www.faithworks.info** or, especially in Northern Ireland, **www.ccwa-ni.org.uk/**.

Discuss with the group how you can serve people in the community around you:
• Think of a target group that you could help, such as children who hang round a certain street, or some older people who live in a care home.
• In what ways can you help them? How do you know what they need?
• What abilities and talents do you have in the group? How much time do you have available?
• What will you need to carry out your act of service? Have you got the equipment you need? Will it cost anything? How will you get the money? Will you need to do some fundraising first?
• When will you do it?
• Where will you do it?
• What jobs need to be done? Share these out as fairly as possible.
• How will you let people know what is happening?

If your group is small and it seems too daunting to take on a community project by yourselves, you could join in with something that the church is already involved in – such as a soup run – or do something for people within the church.

Build in time for feedback after the event. Get young people to talk about what it was like to serve. What have they learned? How has it affected their lives?

# EVENT 8
## FENCING/WORTH FIGHTING FOR

### TARGET

To realise that some things are really worth fighting for – God calls us to fight for the oppressed.

### KEY PASSAGE

Luke 4:14–30

### TRAINING FOR YOU

Luke 3 and 4 are great chapters for introducing Jesus and his ministry. Take some time to read them now, to reacquaint yourself with him – here we see Jesus' baptism and his heavenly family, Jesus' earthly family, his temptation, his announcement of his mission and how he starts to work that out. In this session, we'll be looking at the words Jesus quotes from Isaiah to describe his ministry. What do these words tell you about Jesus? Here he was announcing to the world who he was and what he had come to do. Some didn't want to accept that this Jesus, who they had known for years, was God's Messiah, but others believed. Pray about how the young people in your group might receive Jesus and his mission. Pray that Jesus will have a big impact on their lives, as they see his care for people in all kinds of difficulties.

### FOR YOUNG PEOPLE OUTSIDE A CHURCH COMMUNITY

Depending on the background of the young people in your group, fighting may be an all too prominent reality. However, Jesus' call to turn the world upside-down in the passage from Luke 4, goes against this contemporary fighting. Jesus came to free captives, give sight to the blind and liberate those who have been treated unfairly, not to fight only for your mates, get revenge for others' actions or to gain status or belongings. Challenge the young people to start thinking about what is worth fighting for.

### FOR CHURCH YOUNG PEOPLE

The activity of organisations such as Soul Survivor, Christian Aid and Tearfund in the area of social justice has encouraged a desire in young people to help the poor and oppressed both at home and abroad. Among church young people, that has the added dimension of answering God's call to stand up for the poor. As you go through this session, how can you help church young people start to put their faith into action?

**British Fencing**
www.britishfencing.com

# ASSEMBLY/ BASIC TALK OUTLINE

Aim: to realise that some things are really worth fighting for – God calls us to fight for the oppressed.

## WHAT YOU NEED

• Two trays
• Two rolled-up newspapers

## WHAT YOU DO

Depending on the context, either have a few pairs of challengers or two large teams lined up against each other. Number each pair of opponents so that all pairs have a unique number. Call out a number at random. The two opponents of that number each run to pick up a tray, balance it on one hand, then take their sword (ie the roll of newspaper) in the other. The aim is to knock the opponent's tray from their hand with their sword, while keeping their own tray safe from their opponent. Points are scored when the opponent's tray is knocked over. When one pair has played, repeat the process by calling out another number, until the whole team has played. Keep track of the score.

There is a lot of fighting in the world. Look around and you'll see it – in the playground, in the movies, in the newspapers. We are all natural fighters. As little children we don't need to learn how to argue with people around us. When people hurt us, very often our first response is to feel angry – to confront people and find justice.

There is nothing wrong with fighting. In fact, it can be a noble thing to do. The question is, are we fighting for the right thing? The Bible says that we should 'fight the good fight' – but what does that mean? Very often, what we fight about isn't important. We get overly concerned about people being in the right place in the queue, or people giving us the credit we feel we deserve. Our fighting is motivated by our own sense of pride. But God invites us to fight for the things we see that are wrong in the world. All over the world – on our own doorsteps, in our own communities – people find themselves treated unfairly by people who are stronger than they are. Children are sold and kept in slavery. People feel alone and friendless. Just imagine what would happen if we put aside our own little battles and joined forces to try to tackle all the things which were so obviously wrong around us. We would be unstoppable!

# RESOURCES FOR 11 TO 14S

## IN YOUR OWN WORDS

**Introductory activity**
**For all groups**
**10 minutes**

Aim: to start thinking about what poverty is and who it affects.

### WHAT YOU NEED
- Card
- Pens
- Some music and the means to play it
- String and clothes pegs
- Internet access (optional)

### WHAT YOU DO

As a way of introducing the theme of poverty, ask the group to explain in their own words what poverty is. You could play some background music while they do this.

Hand out some sheets of paper or card. Divide everybody into groups of four or five and get them to write up some definitions for poverty. Give them a few minutes to come up with some ideas and write them down.

Once all the groups have written down some definitions come back together and ask them to share their ideas. Write up keywords on large sheets of card and peg them on a line of string. You will probably get some of the following words: hunger, malnutrition, AIDS, unclean water, Third World, low life expectancy, poor housing, homelessness, street children, no education, unable to read and write.

Ask the group to shout out the names of countries which they think have a huge poverty crisis. They may come up with some of the following, but just try and get a list of about ten countries written down.

The 50 poorest countries in the world: Afghanistan, Angola, Bangladesh, Benin, Bhutan, Burkina Faso, Burundi, Cambodia, Cape Verde, Central African Republic, Chad, Comoros, Democratic Republic of Congo, Djibouti, Equatorial Guinea, Eritrea, Ethiopia, Gambia, Guinea, Guinea-Bissau, Haiti, Kiribati, Lao People's Democratic Republic, Lesotho, Liberia, Madagascar, Malawi, Maldives, Mali, Mauritania, Mozambique, Myanmar, Nepal, Niger, Rwanda, Samoa, São Tomé and Príncipe, Senegal, Sierra Leone, Solomon Islands, Somalia, Sudan, East Timor, Togo, Tuvalu, Uganda, Tanzania, Vanuatu, Yemen, Zambia.

If you have Internet access, try to discover which of these countries have suffered war and conflict in recent years. Chat about what these countries may have been fighting for/against.

## GOD'S HEARTBEAT

**Bible**
**For all groups**
**10 minutes**

Aim: to show that God takes poverty seriously; those suffering injustice matter to him.

### WHAT YOU DO
- Bibles
- Paper and pens
- Images of poverty (from the Internet, newspapers or magazines)

### WHAT YOU DO

Get hold of some images of people living in poverty; maybe use some issues that are currently in the news. Divide the young people into small groups, so you will need enough images for each group.

Get them to describe what they think is going on:
– How do they feel about the images?
– What action needs to be taken/could be taken to help the situation?

Explain that the Bible says a lot about the poor and those living in need of justice and mercy. God's heart beats with compassion for the needy. The suffering of those living in poverty isn't something ignored by God. He sees the suffering… and he also wants to see people act to respond, to alleviate injustice. Ask the groups to look up these Bible verses: Micah 6:8; Isaiah 61:1,2; Proverbs 31:8,9; James 1:27; Isaiah 1:17

You could spilt the group into pairs or threes and give each small group one or two of these references to look up.

What do the verses tell us about God's attitude to the poor? What do the verses say should be our attitude and response to the poor?

# RAISING THE ISSUE

**Bible**
**For church groups**
**15 minutes**

Aim: to see how Jesus was really concerned for the poor and the needy.

## WHAT YOU NEED

• Bibles
• Paper and pens

## WHAT YOU DO

To go along with this activity you could get hold of some stories of real young people living in poverty. Organisations such as Tearfund and Christian Aid would be able to provide you with some real life examples (**www.tearfund.org** and **www. christianaid.org.uk**).

As a group, read Luke 4:14–30. This is about Jesus in his hometown. At first, the crowd was amazed at his wise teaching – after all, news about Jesus was pretty positive – but very soon the people in the synagogue were outraged. Ask the young people to imagine they are in the crowd listening to Jesus. How would they have felt listening to Jesus? Excited? Angry? Bored? Would his words have inspired them to imitate him in reaching out to the poor and oppressed?

Discuss these questions together:
• Why do you think Jesus quoted some verses from the Old Testament, from Isaiah 61:1,2?
• What do you think these verses mean?
• What kind of challenge do they present us as followers of Jesus?

# GET BUSY

**Response**
**For all groups**
**10 minutes**

Aim: to challenge the group to take action on poverty.

## WHAT YOU NEED

• Sword shapes cut from silver card
• Felt-tip pens
• Resources from a number of charities such as Tearfund, World Vision and Christian Aid
• A large sheet of paper

## WHAT YOU DO

Spend a few minutes praying for some of the big issues facing those living in poverty. As you pray, try and get the group to imagine what it's like to have no home, no education, only dirty water to drink, being constantly sick etc. Write some of these emotions and problems on the sword shapes. Then, using these 'swords' as a stimulus, encourage the members of the group to pray short prayers out loud. If this isn't appropriate for your group, get them to reflect quietly.

As a group, talk about what action you could take to help tackle poverty. It is a big daunting task, but something we can't choose to ignore. Decide here and now to take action! Make a commitment.

Encourage people to share some ideas. Write these ideas down on a large sheet of paper. If the group is stuck for ideas, share some of the following:
• Raise money for charities working against poverty. Many have online gift catalogues where you can buy people things like goats and rabbits! Or take part in something like World Vision's 24-hour fast.
• Sponsor a child living in poverty; this is something Compassion UK and World Vision do. It's a commitment of approximately £18 a month and the money goes towards sponsoring a specific child's community. You can usually write to the child as well.
• Fairtrade. Think about what you buy and why. Fairtrade products include many different items such as chocolate, coffee, tea, bananas and honey. Look out for the Fairtrade logo on items. Tearfund and other charities helping the poor, have good resources: check out **www.tearfund.org/youth**
• Pray. Pray for people living in poverty. Get hold of prayer resources from a number of different charities.
• Get practical. You might live near or in a deprived area. Find out what needs there are and see what, as a group, you can do.

# RESOURCES FOR 14 TO 18S

## THAT'S SO UNFAIR

**Introductory activity**
**For all groups**
**10 minutes**

Aim: to get the group thinking about unfairness.

### WHAT YOU NEED

• Wrapped presents for your group (eg different sizes of chocolate bar – some 'fun-size' bars, some medium-size bars, and a few large bars, you will need slightly fewer bars than the number of people in your group)

### WHAT YOU DO

Tell the group you've got presents for them all. Hand out the different sized chocolate bars randomly around the group – some people will not have one. Sit back and watch the reactions – the activity will run itself!

After a while, steer the discussion towards questions, such as:
• How does it feel to have less?
• How does it feel to have more?
• How does it feel to have nothing?
• How do you think God feels about unfairness?

## GETTING STUCK IN

**Bible**
**For all groups**
**20 minutes**

Aim: to focus on Jesus' manifesto for his ministry and see what that means for us.

### WHAT YOU NEED

• Paper and pens
• Bibles

### WHAT YOU DO

What is it that your group feels is worth fighting for? Get some responses, and write some of the ideas down on paper. Split the young people into two smaller groups and ask one group to look at Luke 4:14–30 and the other to look at Amos 5:10–12. Each group should decide what the speaker (God, via Amos, and Jesus) says about their mission. Make a list of their thoughts.

Bring the group back together to compare the lists – what are the similarities? Then compare these things with the first list that the group wrote down: what's worth fighting for. How do the group's initial responses shape up against these two Bible passages?

What does this tell you about Jesus? What is his character like? What does this tell you about God's priorities? The passage highlights the fact that the people of Israel were full of selfishness, greed and injustice. As they became more and more affluent, they began to take advantage of the poor. If the poor owed money, they were forced to sell their homes to pay the bill. If the poor wanted justice in court, they would have to pay a bribe to the judge. This is how the people of Israel 'walked' over the poor – they were not following God's 'heart' for them.

This is maybe not a million miles from how the poor are treated today by those of us who are rich. How does God want us to respond? How does God want us to treat those in poverty? Instead of walking all over the poor, how can we help them to get back on their feet?

Jesus said: 'The Lord has put his Spirit in me, because he appointed me to tell the Good News to the poor' (Luke 4:18). How can we tell 'good news' to poor people? Is 'telling good news' always about using words?

# LITERAL/SPIRITUAL

**Bible**
**For church groups**
**10 minutes**

Aim: to use Jesus' words to reflect on what is worth fighting for.

## WHAT YOU NEED

• Large sheets of paper
• Marker pens
• Bibles

## WHAT YOU DO

Think together for a while about things that can be both literal, but have another meaning. There are many phrases in Christian jargon that have a literal and more spiritual meaning. For example, what meanings are there for 'good news' or 'Jesus in my heart'? Go on to ask what the young people understand by the words 'worth fighting for'. They might think about physical fighting, or a more figurative idea of the word 'fight' – to pursue with passion, to champion.

Read Luke 4:14–30 together and then split the group into pairs or threes. Give each pair/three a sheet of paper and a pen, and ask them to split the page into two columns. At the top of one column, write 'literal' and the other 'spiritual'. Go through Jesus' words in verses 18 and 19 and write a literal meaning for his words, then think about another more spiritual or figurative meaning that these might have.

When everyone has finished, get feedback on what they have written. You might have suggestions, such as who the spiritual poor might be, the spiritually blind, or those held captive by addiction or circumstance, rather than being physically imprisoned.

What does this tell the young people about Jesus' mission? If you have time, you might want to look at some other passages, such as Luke 4:31–37 or Matthew 9:27–38. How do Jesus' words apply here?

How can we 'fight for' people like this today? Get some suggestions from the group and then go on to the response activity.

# MAKING A DIFFERENCE

**Response**
**For all groups**
**20 minutes**

Aim: to help the group to start 'fighting for' these causes.

## WHAT YOU NEED

• Paper and pens

## WHAT YOU DO

It's all very well feeling challenged about the poverty around us, but we need to act on this in real ways. This section gives your group the chance to do this.
• Do they and their families buy fairly traded goods whenever possible?
• Do their schools use Fairtrade food in the canteen?
• Are the teachers drinking Fairtrade coffee in the staff room?
• What shops do we buy our clothes from?
• Do we know whether these shops have 'ethical policies' regarding what they pay their workers? If not, how can we find out?

One reason that poverty exists in our world is because of the low wages and prices often paid to the producers of the goods we buy. The developed nations often exploit producers of coffee, cocoa, etc.

Suggest that the group writes letters to their school/college head teachers, asking them to consider making their schools a 'Fairtrade' zone – using as many fairly traded products as possible. And suggest that the group thinks more carefully about the clothes shops they buy from – cheap clothes may mean underpaid workers!

You could also organise a Fairtrade stall showcasing Fairtrade products to people in your church community, or in a local community centre or hub. Contact local shops or supermarkets to see if they will help you, or check out the Fairtrade website: **www.fairtrade.org.uk**. They also have other ways to get involved.

Organisations such as Christian Aid (**www.christianaid.org.uk/getinvolved**) and World Vision (**www.worldvision.org.uk**) have other ideas to help young people fight for the poor and persecuted.

# EVENT 9
## MARATHON/WITH GOD FOR LIFE!

### TARGET
To understand that following Jesus isn't a quick sprint, but a race for life – we need to persevere, even when life is tough!

### KEY PASSAGE
Hebrews 12:1–3

### TRAINING FOR YOU
How is your spiritual journey at the moment? Are you struggling? Or are you doing well? This session will help young people start to understand the commitment and perseverance that is required when following Jesus, and your testimony will be helpful to the young people, as they see a Christian coping with the ups and downs of life, but keeping their eyes fixed on Jesus. Think about the times in your life where you have had to persevere – or are there times when you gave up? Bring these times to God now, and ask him to help you in the future as you continue to walk with him.

### FOR YOUNG PEOPLE OUTSIDE A CHURCH COMMUNITY
Today's culture is to give up on something when it doesn't work out. You see it with friendships, relationships, on soap operas, in the gossip mags. There aren't that many examples of people sticking at things. In this 'now' culture, it is easier to cut and run, rather than work towards a greater benefit further down the line. It is in this culture that all young people are growing up, but young people from outside a church community are likely to have been less exposed to the idea of sticking at something that has become difficult. They may also hold the idea that when you become a Christian, everything is then sorted. As you work with these young people, be aware of this culture and help them to see the prize that Paul talks about in Philippians 3.

### FOR CHURCH YOUNG PEOPLE
Church young people will understand a bit more the idea that following Jesus isn't going to be a bed of roses and that the need to stick at it. However, this cut-and-run attitude is still held by some in church (how many people have you seen moving because of some perceived slight they have received from another church member or the minister?). Help these young people to see how great the prize is for sticking with Jesus – this is where your own story can be powerful this session.

**UK Athletics**
www.uka.org.uk
**British Triathlon Federation**
www.britishtriathlon.org

# ASSEMBLY/ BASIC TALK OUTLINE

Aim: to understand that following Jesus isn't a quick sprint, but a race for life – we need to persevere, even when life is tough!

## WHAT YOU NEED

- Watermelons
- A stopwatch
- A small prize
- Clean-up and cover-up facilities
- Pictures of people competing in endurance events (optional)

## WHAT YOU DO

Before the assembly or session, make sure you cover up the area where you'll be playing the game.

Ask for four or five volunteers and invite them to your playing area. Explain that you are going to have a watermelon marathon, and show the prize you have for the winner. Give each player a watermelon and say that, when you give the signal, each player has to hold their watermelon out in front of them, with arms outstretched. Everyone has to continue to hold out their watermelon until they can do so no longer. When they've reached their limit, they should drop the watermelon on the floor. If the fruit smashes, it will make quite a mess, so make sure you provide enough protection for the players and the spectators close to the action. (If you want to do a cleaner version of this game, then use basketballs or medicine balls. However, the messy version will be more memorable in the minds of the young people!)

Record the time of the player who holds out the longest, and award the winner the prize. Ask each competitor how they felt during the game. Did they feel like giving up? What kept them going? Did they think they were going to win?

Go on to talk about other endurance events, such as triathlon or road cycling, and in particular, the marathon. You might want to show pictures of people competing in these disciplines, if you have them. What do the young people think makes athletes want to compete in such difficult sports?

Like endurance events, following Christ is something that needs endurance and perseverance. There are times when we might feel like giving up, when life is difficult and things aren't going our way. But Christians run on, looking towards the prize – an everlasting life with Jesus.

For Christians, this is the best prize ever. A man called Paul, who was one of the first leaders of the church, wrote a letter to Christians in the town of Philippi in Greece. He told them, 'Brothers and sisters, I know that I have not yet reached that goal, but there is one thing I always do. Forgetting the past and straining towards what is ahead, I keep trying to reach the goal and get the prize for which God called me through Christ to the life above.'

Paul was running a difficult marathon, but he persevered and had his eyes firmly on the prize – an eternal life with Jesus.

# RESOURCES FOR 11 TO 14S

## WORK OUT
**Introductory activity**
**For all groups**
**15 minutes**

Aim: to begin looking at the theme of perseverance and realising how much effort and commitment is needed to keep going.

## WHAT YOU NEED
- Flip-chart paper
- Marker pens

## WHAT YOU DO
Tell your group that it's time to get energetic. Then lead them through the following routine:
- Ten sit-ups
- Ten press-ups
- Running on the spot for one minute
- Ten star jumps

Repeat as desired… and watch what happens – some of the group will no doubt drop out!

Stop the activity and get everyone to sit down:
- How easy was it to persevere?
- How easy was it to quit?
- What do you think it takes to be a very fit athlete?

Hopefully the group will come up with suggestions like the following: hard work, effort, commitment, dedication, determination, perseverance.

Ask the group: 'When you think of the word "perseverance", what words spring to mind?' Write the young people's responses down. Use this to introduce the theme for the session.

Now share the story of athlete, Paula Radcliffe:
At the Athens Olympics in 2004 Paula Radcliffe was the hot favourite to win gold in the marathon. But in the overbearing Athens heat, Paula Radcliffe's dreams of gold ended when she retired from the race after 23 miles. You can probably remember seeing TV pictures of Paula distraught sitting by the roadside. The moment when she was overtaken and dropped to fourth place, something gave up inside of her… she couldn't keep going…

Things went much better for Paula when she destroyed her rivals to win her third London Marathon title in 2 hours, 17 minutes and 42 seconds. Her winning time was the fastest ever in a women's-only race, beating the previous best of 2:18:56 she set on her debut in 2002.

Later, she set the world record of 2:15:25 when she ran with the men, but insisted that victory – her fifth international marathon win – was the main goal that time.

'It was about winning again,' she added. 'A lot of people thought that after what happened in Athens I was never going to be the same again.'

Finally, discuss the following questions:
- How would you describe Paula Radcliffe's attitude and actions?
- What has kept her going?
- Are there other sports people, or people in general, that you admire because they have shown great perseverance?

## MARATHON RUNNING
**Bible**
**For all groups**
**10 minutes**

Aim: to help the young people to understand that being a Christian is for life and we need to commit to the long haul.

## WHAT YOU NEED
- Bibles
- Paper and pens

## WHAT YOU DO
Split the young people into small groups and ask them to put together a list of the kind of training needed to run a marathon.

Here are some ideas:
- Training will require running in the cold and wet, and on dark nights or mornings.
- Training takes up a lot of time. Your regular lifestyle may need changing to fit in marathon training.
- You need to eat the right kind of food to give your body energy to burn.

• You need to build up to running a marathon – do some 5k, 10k, half-marathon runs.
• Gradually build up the mileage.

Ask the young people to consider in their groups whether it is easy or difficult to follow Jesus. What things do they think they might struggle with? (The answers here will be very different depending on the background of the young people in your group.)

Now read Hebrews 12:1–3. Make the point that the Christian life is described as a race. It's not really a 100-metre sprint, but a long-haul marathon. The end prize is fantastic, but the race is not always easy. We have to train!

Ask the groups to read Mark 8:34–36 and Matthew 7:13,14 and summarise what they think Jesus is communicating about the challenge of following him. Make the point that Jesus never promised his followers an easy ride. Being a Christian isn't for the faint hearted; it requires guts and determination to keep going, whatever experiences we face.

There are times when we get lost. We feel too weary to go on. We might even fall and collapse. We may want to give up, walk away and turn back. But whatever you do, hang in there and keep going – persevere. You're not alone in the struggle; every Christian experiences hard times.

Finally, ask the young people to consider the kind of things that they should do to help them persevere in the marathon race of following Jesus. How does what they have said in response to the opening question in this activity relate to following Jesus?

## PROMOTING PERSEVERANCE
**Response**
**For all groups**
**5 minutes**

Aim: to help young people to consider some practical steps to perseverance.

### WHAT YOU NEED
• Poster-making materials, eg paper, pens, paint

### WHAT YOU DO
Tell the group that they have to come up with a poster to promote and encourage the importance of perseverance using the lessons they have learned in this session. Help them by telling them that the 'Pocket Penguin Thesaurus' associates the following words with 'perseverance' – 'continue, persist, carry on, go on, keep going, struggle on, soldier on, plug away, stick at, endure, hold fast'. Maybe they could parody the famous World War II poster, 'Keep Calm and Carry On'!

You could judge the winning entry and perhaps produce multiple copies of it for each young person to take home and put on their wall as a reminder to persevere.

Offer the following further helpful ideas:
• One way in which we grow and keep going as Christians is to spend time with Jesus. Encourage the group to pray each morning committing the day to God and 'talking' to him about everyday issues in our lives.
• Another thing we need to do to keep close to Jesus is to read the Bible. Encourage the group to follow some kind of Bible reading plan or use daily Bible reading notes.
• Encourage the group to keep each other accountable for remaining committed.
• Invite the young people to pray (in their heads or out loud) about the areas in their lives where they need greater commitment and perseverance. If they prefer, give them time to write their own prayers which they can read out loud.

Close by praying that God will help each of them in these areas.

# RESOURCES FOR 14 TO 18S

## GOING THE DISTANCE

**Introductory activity**
**For all groups**
**10 minutes**

Aim: to think about endurance and perseverance, and how we need that in various activities in life.

## WHAT YOU NEED

- Pictures or video clips of different sporting events that require endurance, such as marathon, triathlon, open-water swimming, cross-country skiing, round the world yacht racing – the more extreme the better!
- A laptop and Internet access (if using YouTube or other video website to show clips)
- Paper and marker pen

## WHAT YOU DO

Gather together your pictures or clips of endurance sports (searching for 'Endurance sports' in Wikipedia is a good place to start, though not mentioned, there is the Marathon des Sables: (**www.darbaroud.com**). Show the young people the pictures or clips and then discuss what might be the most difficult sport to take part in.

Rank the events in order of difficulty and the amount of endurance that would be needed to complete the event. Are there any events that the young people would want to take part in?

What kind of endurance do we need to live our daily lives? Are there parts of our lives that are as difficult as some of these events? Get some feedback, and if any young people are willing to give examples from their lives, then let them do so, but encourage the rest of the group to be positive and affirming, rather than allowing them to judge or ridicule in any way.

## RUNNING THE RACE

**Bible**
**For all groups**
**25 minutes**

Aim: to illustrate the importance of commitment and perseverance in following Jesus.

## WHAT YOU NEED

- A large sheet of paper
- Marker pens

## WHAT YOU DO

Ask the group to name some of their sporting heroes. Write down the names they call out on the paper. You may want to add your own too!

Discuss the following questions with your group:
- What makes these people sporting heroes?
- What do they have in common?
- How have they achieved their success?

In the world of sport, there are few great athletes to whom success has come easily. The people who rise to the top of their game are usually distinguished by a drive to work hard and determination to reach their goals. Chat for a moment about some of the training that these sportspeople have to put in.

The apostle Paul often spoke of the Christian life as a race. Read 1 Corinthians 9:24–27.
- What do you think is the 'prize' which Paul encourages us to aim for?
- What sort of 'training' could help us in our race?
- How can we 'run in such a way as to get the prize'?

The ultimate prize we are promised as Christians is eternal life with God, in a world where suffering and death no longer exist. The path to this is one of following Christ, and becoming more like him. This requires the commitment and perseverance of an athlete – it is a lifelong challenge. However, we are not required to meet this challenge alone – many others are running the same race with us. Jesus himself shared our experience of being human in order that we might have a role model for our 'training'.

Read Hebrews 12:1–3 and discuss:
• What are the things that make it difficult for you to follow Jesus?
• What can you do about this?

Invite your group to discuss or think about the following:
• What are your goals in life?
• Who are your role models?
• What one thing could you do every day to move nearer to your goal?
• How does God fit in to your plans?

## COST AND PURPOSE

**Bible**
**For church groups**
**10 minutes**

Aim: to encourage the young people to think about the commitment and perseverance that is required to follow Christ.

### WHAT YOU NEED

• Bibles

### WHAT YOU DO

Split the young people into small groups and give out the Bibles. Ask them to discuss in their groups how they feel about doing something when they know that it will cost them dearly in time, money or effort.

Now ask them how they would feel if there was a bigger purpose to what they were doing. For example, going shopping for their gran takes up their spare time and effort, but because gran can't get out it means that she will have food for the week and a visit from someone.

Ask them to read Matthew 8:18–22. When they have done this, ask them to discuss the following questions:
• What do you think about this passage?
• What does this passage tell you about following Jesus and how it will affect your life?
• What does this teach you about commitment and perseverance and being a Christian?

Ask for each group to feed back some of their answers. Sum up the activity by reading Hebrews 12:1–3 and commenting that it takes a lot of commitment and perseverance to follow Jesus, but that there is an ultimate purpose and gift at the end of it – spending all eternity in heaven with a loving heavenly Father.

## DAILY ENCOURAGEMENT

**Response**
**For all groups**
**10 minutes**

Aim: to learn some verses about perseverance to help remind the group about living for Jesus.

### WHAT YOU NEED

• Bibles
• Assorted resources such as paper and pens, art materials, musical instruments – whatever might help your group learn Bible verses.

### WHAT YOU DO

If your group has grown up in church, they will have learned memory verses already and be familiar with the concept. If not, explain that it is helpful sometimes to learn small parts of the Bible so that, when you're struggling, you have some of God's Word to draw on!

Read these verses out to the group: Philippians 3:13b,14 and Hebrews 12:1. Let the young people choose one of those verses to learn, and help them decide how they are going to memorise it. You could make a poster, make up a song, design actions to perform alongside saying the verse, make a reminder in the form of a credit card-shaped card to fit in their wallet.

When everyone is ready, show and perform your memory aides to the rest of the group. During the week, you could also text, tweet or facebook these verses to each other (ensuring that appropriate safeguarding guidelines are kept, of course).

# DECATHLON EVENT 10

## GYMNASTICS / LIVING FOR GOD NOW

### TARGET

To understand that we can follow Jesus, and make a difference in the world, now – we don't have to wait!

### KEY PASSAGE

1 Samuel 16:1–13

### TRAINING FOR YOU

We know that we shouldn't judge people on superficial terms, but sometimes it's hard not to be impressed by appearances, as Samuel is here. Think about the young people in your group – by what criteria does society judge them? A young person's worth is all too often weighed by their appearance and attitude, not by who they are or what they can contribute. What emotional baggage might they be carrying because of these judgements? Now think about how you judge them. Is that different from the way they are judged by others? God's method of judging people's character is clear – he looks on the inside (1 Samuel 13:7) and sees their potential. Does the way we assess character match God's way?

### FOR YOUNG PEOPLE OUTSIDE A CHURCH COMMUNITY

Young people in our society are often marginalised. They are demonised by the media, most of which seem convinced that there is a young person with a knife around every corner. Young people from outside a church community may be surprised that Jesus is interested in them, that they can follow him now and that they can make a difference – that God uses young people as much as everyone else! Do your best to facilitate young people in their exploration of these points during this session.

### FOR CHURCH YOUNG PEOPLE

Church young people may not have had the chance to minister in their church setting before. Churches can be unwilling sometimes to let young people perform some of the same ministries as adults. As you go through this session (and reflect on previous sessions), try to identify areas where your young people are passionate, have skills and might have opportunities to serve the wider church. And then try to make this possible!

**British Gymnastics**
www.british-gymnastics.org

# ASSEMBLY/ BASIC TALK OUTLINE

Aim: to understand that we can follow Jesus, and make a difference in the world, now – we don't have to wait!

## WHAT YOU NEED

- A range of props, eg balls (various sizes from tennis ball to beach ball), ribbons, hula hoops, rope or clubs/batons
- Sound system
- A playlist made up of different rhythms and genres
- Roll/gym mats

## WHAT YOU DO

Before the session, put together a playlist made up of different rhythms and genres. You could use some of these songs, or others that you know your young people are familiar with: 'It's Like That' Run DMC, 'Call On Me' Eric Prydz, 'Cha Cha Slide' DJ Casper, 'New York' Alicia Keyes, 'Children' Robert Miles, 'Ride of the Valkyries' Wagner, 'Sorcerer's Apprentice' Dukas, 'Blaze of Glory' Jon Bon Jovi, 'Feel Good Inc' Gorillaz, 'Smiley Faces' Gnarls Barkley

This activity can be used with either a few volunteers or an entire class, depending on the context. Warm the young people up with some quality gymnastics moves, such as forward and backward rolls, cartwheels, handstands, run and jump. Introduce some of the props and invite the young people to use them in their routine.

Play some of the music. Invite the young people to create their own routine to the music. Depending on the context, it may be sensible to limit this to a one-minute routine, or have all young people performing simultaneously on different mats. Invite some other volunteers to act as judges, awarding marks for musicality, creativity and energy.

Nadia Comaneci performed in the gymnastics events at the 1976 Montreal Olympic Games and won three gold medals. She was so good, she scored the first ever *perfect 10* in Olympic gymnastics. And she was only 14 years old.

How often are you told that you're too young to make decisions? How often are we led to believe that what we're doing now is preparation for 'life' which will happen at some point later? The truth is, young people all over the world achieve remarkable things. They are living life now, not waiting for the future.

There are some letters in the Bible between a wise man named Paul and a young church leader called Timothy. In one of these letters, Paul tells Timothy, 'Do not let anyone treat you as if you are unimportant because you are young. Instead, be an example to the believers with your words, your actions, your love, your faith, and your pure life' (1 Timothy 4:12).

You don't need to wait until you are an adult to make decisions about your life. You can't use the excuse of being young as a reason to not achieve things today.

Jesus makes an offer to every person, young or old, to live life his way and to do incredible things as a result. It's up to you to decide what you do with this, now.

# RESOURCES FOR 11 TO 14S

## I DREAM A DREAM

**Introductory activity**
**For all groups**
**15 minutes**

Aim: to introduce the theme that God has a plan for each of us, and that we don't need to wait until we are older to respond to his call.

## WHAT YOU NEED

• *Kung Fu Panda* DVD
• A DVD player and TV or laptop and projector
• A large sheet of paper
• Pens
• Post-it® notes
• YouTube clips of interviews with gymnasts (optional)
• A laptop and Internet access (optional)

## WHAT YOU DO

At the beginning of the session, stick up a large sheet of paper with the words 'I dream a dream' as the headline.

Tell the young people they are going to watch the very beginning of the film, *Kung Fu Panda*. For those who haven't seen the film, say that Po is an ordinary panda working in a noodle restaurant who dreams of being the biggest kung-fu warrior ever. Play the clip (from 00:00:36 to 00:02:25).

If there are young people present who have seen the film, ask them to explain how the story develops. Bizarre as it seems, when you look at Po, he does eventually become that kung-fu warrior he dreams about – but it doesn't happen quite as easily as it does in his dreams!

Give each of the young people some Post-it® notes and ask them to write down any hopes or dreams they have for the future. Reassure them that these can be big or small, realistic or beyond their wildest dreams. Ask them to write their name on each of their Post-it® notes.

As the young people do this, encourage them to talk to each other about what they're writing. Encourage leaders to interact as well – maybe they could write up some of their own dreams and hopes.

You could, at this point get the young people to watch an interview or two with gymnasts, talking about their dreams and how they are working towards them now. Interviews with the US gymnast, Shawn Johnson, are particularly pertinent here. What do the young people think of these gymnasts' dreams?

The important thing to remember is that God does have a plan for every person's life – it may not be quite as spectacular as some of the dreams written up on the wall, of those of the gymnasts, but it may be even more spectacular!

## FROM SHEPHERD BOY TO KING

**Bible**
**For all groups**
**20 minutes**

Aim: to show that David's calling was unmistakable, despite being young.

## WHAT YOU NEED

• Bibles
• Paper and pens

## WHAT YOU DO

Ask the young people to imagine for the moment that they have been chosen to do something extremely important. It's a top job. Ask for someone to volunteer what job they're thinking of and get them to stand up.

Now ask if anyone else's imagined role or job is more important – listen to their answer and leave the one who you say has the more important job standing. Continue until there are no more challenges and congratulate your young person on his most prestigious job.

Say that you are going to be reading about someone in the Bible who ended up with the top job. It wasn't a job he would even have dared to dream about, and even the person who gave him the job thought at first it was going to someone else.

Read 1 Samuel 16:1–13 together. You might need to explain that King Saul was no longer obedient to God, so the time had come for God to choose a new king. Although David is anointed at this time by Samuel with olive oil (a practice which continues as our Queen was also anointed with oil at her coronation), he will not become king until Saul dies.

Having read the story through and ensured that everyone understands it, ask the young people to re-enact the story dramatically, working in small groups. Ask them to try and get across the feelings of the different characters, eg the elders, Jesse, Eliab, Abinadab, Shammah, Samuel – they may have to imagine some of their feelings because they are not clearly stated in the Bible passage.

Once everyone has had time to prepare, watch the dramas. Ask the group: 'Were there any insights from the dramas that helped to shed more light on the Bible story?'

Finish by saying that up to the point of Samuel's visit, David would have had no idea that he would be king of Israel. He probably imagined a sheep-filled future with some harp-playing and songwriting, and the killing of the occasional bear or lion. However, when Samuel anoints him, there is no denying that God has another purpose for his life. He hears the call and, as we read more about his life in the Bible, we know that David was obedient to God's call and willingly became the next king of Israel.

Once he was king, life did not become easy for David, nor did he always make right or godly decisions, but ultimately he always came back to God, repented of his mistakes and desired to put God first.

David's calling was unmistakable – it involved the chief prophet, a horn of olive oil, and being chosen above all his brothers. Our calling may not be so obvious, but we can take encouragement from the fact that God looks at each person's heart, and has a plan for each person's life.

## NOT TOO YOUNG
**Response**
**For all groups**
**10 minutes**

Aim: to create a reminder that God can use people whatever their age.

### WHAT YOU NEED
- Travel mirrors or mirror tiles
- Glass pens or small pieces of card and pens
- Copies of Jeremiah 1:7,8

### WHAT YOU DO
Travel or mirror tiles can be purchased quite cheaply, but if you are unable to find any you could use pieces of card instead, covered in foil or reflective paper. You will need to put masking tape around the edges of the mirror tiles, if you are using them.

Give out the copies of the verses from Jeremiah 1 and say the verses together: 'The Lord said to me, "Don't say, 'I am only a boy.' You must go everywhere I send you, and you must say everything I tell you to say. Don't be afraid of anyone, because I am with you to protect you," says the Lord' (Jeremiah 1:7,8).

Ask the young people to write the verse out on a travel mirror or mirror tile, which they can keep in their bedroom as a reminder that God can use them whatever their age. Alternatively, they can write the verse on a piece of card and stick it up near their mirror at home.

# RESOURCES FOR 14 TO 18S

## WHAT DOES IT DO?

**Introductory activity**
**For all groups**
**20 minutes**

Aim: to introduce the idea that God has a calling for everyone and that God's way is ultimately best, even though it may not always appear so immediately.

### WHAT YOU NEED

• Unusual objects
• Hand-held mirrors

### WHAT YOU DO

Before the session, challenge each of your leaders and/or the young people to bring along a really unusual object or gadget. In turn, they present the object and everyone else has to try and guess what its purpose is. What was it designed for? Congratulate any who guess correctly.

Thank those who have brought in things, then hand round the mirrors and ask the young people to look into them. As they do so they need to ask a similar question – what are they designed for? What does God want them to do with their lives?

Now ask if any of the young people have any ideas on what they want to do in the future. Listen to their thoughts. You could ask if anyone wants to talk about their God-given talents (if you have done Event 6).

Explain that in this session they will be thinking about how God has plans for each one of them. They will be hearing of people in the Bible to whom God spoke and who were obedient in doing what God wanted them to do. In some cases this meant that they achieved far more than they would have believed possible, before God spoke to them. Go on to tell this story:

There was a man called Jim Elliot who lived about fifty years ago. He and four friends went to Ecuador to tell a tribe living in the jungle about Jesus. Even though they got to meet some members of the tribe, they were all killed with spears by a group of tribesmen. The tribesmen couldn't work out why the white men didn't defend themselves with the guns that they had with them, and because of this they allowed Jim's widow and his cousin to live and work with them. His son, who was only five when his dad was killed, is also devoting his life to the same tribe.

Jim Elliot said, 'God always gives his best to those who leave the choice with him.' Jim Elliot listened to God, did what he knew God was telling him, and ended up giving his own life – but his family bears no grudges, believing that Jim is now in heaven and that it's their mission to carry on with the work he started.

The leader of the group who killed Jim and his friends is now an old man in his 80s. He is a Christian, he knows he is forgiven, and he is looking forward to meeting Jim and the others in heaven.

## GOD CALLED ME TO...

**Introductory activity**
**For all groups**
**20 minutes**

Aim: to introduce the idea that God has a special call on all of our lives, and to grasp the amazing things that can happen when we respond and serve him.

### WHAT YOU NEED

• Visiting speaker

### WHAT YOU DO

Invite someone to come and speak to the group about something that God called them to do. It would be best if it were a young person who felt that God had called them to serve him in some way or another – through mission work at home or abroad – as this would be really easy for the group to relate to.

You could ask someone who left an incredible job and life to serve as a missionary abroad, with all the uncertainties of where their next meal would come from etc.

Gather the group together and invite your visiting speaker to share what happened in their lives, how they heard God calling them and how they responded. Encourage them to be really honest with the group – if they struggled with what God was asking them to do, get them to say how they wrestled with God's call. Young people like to know that they are not alone when they struggle with what God tells them to do.

Afterwards, encourage the group to ask questions to try and understand what it means to respond to God when he calls us to do something specific and special for him. If your group is not very confident, provide pens and paper. Get them to write their questions down and then give them to your speaker to answer them.

## GO AND MAKE DISCIPLES

**Bible**
**For all groups**
**20 minutes**

Aim: to help the young people to understand what Jesus called his disciples (and us) to do with our lives.

### WHAT YOU NEED

• Bibles
• Pens and paper

### WHAT YOU DO

Explain that people often spend a long time searching for the meaning of life, but Jesus said something to his disciples before he went up to heaven that could answer this question quite clearly. As a group, read Matthew 28:16–20.

Jesus tells his disciples quite clearly what they (and we) are meant to do with our lives – we are to tell other people about Jesus and about his love, forgiveness and salvation, when we have discovered it for ourselves.

Ask the group to split themselves into pairs and to discuss the following questions. Depending on the make up of your group, you will get a variety of answers. Young people from outside a church community may react very differently to those from church. Let the discussion flow, and only step in if things get difficult:
• What do you think of this passage?
• How does it make you feel?
• Is it relevant to you in your life today?
• Is the wording relevant to society today? Is it easy to understand?
• What does it make you want to do?

Give out the pens and paper and ask the groups to rewrite these words of Jesus in more modern language so that they are easier to understand and more relevant to young people today.

After a bit of time, gather them together again and ask them to share what they have written down.

## HOW?

**Response**
**For all groups**
**10 minutes**

Aim: to encourage the young people to think about how they can fulfil God's calling for their lives and to actually do it!

### WHAT YOU NEED

• Paper and pens

### WHAT YOU DO

Split the young people into groups of threes or fours and ask them to discuss what they have learned during this session.

Explain that Jesus charged his disciples with the job of 'making disciples', but how did they do it? How were they meant to do it? Now ask the group to discuss how we are meant to do this today in our lives, in order to fulfil God's calling on us.

Get them to come up with ways that they can reveal Jesus to other young people, children and adults that they know, and to write them down.

After a few minutes, gather together and share ideas. You may like to put some of them into action, so that the group can do what they have learned about, rather than just discuss it.

# RESOURCE PAGE

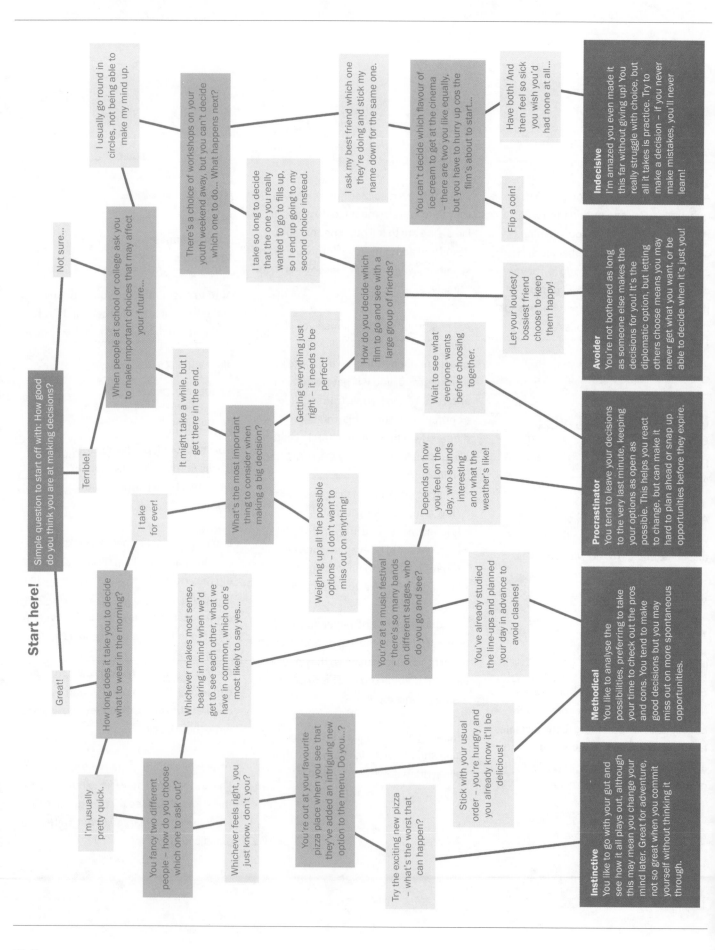

**Start here!**

Simple question to start off with: How good do you think you are at making decisions?

Great!

Not sure....

Terrible!

How long does it take you to decide what to wear in the morning?

I'm usually pretty quick.

I take for ever!

When people at school or college ask you to make important choices that may affect your future...

I usually go round in circles, not being able to make my mind up.

There's a choice of workshops on your youth weekend away, but you can't decide which one to do... What happens next?

It might take a while, but I get there in the end.

I take so long to decide that the one you really wanted to go to fills up, so I end up going to my second choice instead.

I ask my best friend which one they're doing and stick my name down for the same one.

You can't decide which flavour of ice cream to get at the cinema – there are two you like equally, but you have to hurry up cos the film's about to start...

Have both! And then feel so sick you wish you'd had none at all...

Flip a coin!

What's the most important thing to consider when making a big decision?

Getting everything just right – it needs to be perfect!

How do you decide which film to go and see with a large group of friends?

Wait to see what everyone wants before choosing together.

Let your loudest/ bossiest friend choose to keep them happy!

You fancy two different people – how do you choose which one to ask out?

Whichever makes most sense, bearing in mind when we'd get to see each other, what we have in common, which one's most likely to say yes...

Whichever feels right, you just know, don't you?

Weighing up all the possible options – I don't want to miss out on anything!

Depends on how you feel on the day, who sounds interesting and what the weather's like!

You're at a music festival – there's so many bands on different stages, who do you go and see?

You've already studied the line-ups and planned your day in advance to avoid clashes!

You're out at your favourite pizza place when you see that they've added an intriguing new option to the menu. Do you...?

Try the exciting new pizza – what's the worst that can happen?

Stick with your usual order – you're hungry and you already know it'll be delicious!

## Indecisive
I'm amazed you even made it this far without giving up! You really struggle with choice, but all it takes is practice. Try to make a decision – if you never make mistakes, you'll never learn!

## Avoider
You're not bothered as long as someone else makes the decisions for you! It's the diplomatic option, but letting others choose means you may never get what you want, or be able to decide when it's just you!

## Procrastinator
You tend to leave your decisions to the very last minute, keeping your options as open as possible. This helps you react to change, but can make it hard to plan ahead or snap up opportunities before they expire.

## Methodical
You like to analyse the possibilities, preferring to take your time to check out the pros and cons. You tend to make good decisions but you may miss out on more spontaneous opportunities.

## Instinctive
You like to go with your gut and see how it all plays out, although this may mean you change your mind later. Great for adventure, not so great when you commit yourself without thinking it through.

74

# RESOURCE PAGE

## KNOCK

Jesus said, 'Knock and the door will open for you' (Matthew 7:7).

Close your eyes and imagine a closed door. What do you think is behind it?

We cannot know what is behind a closed door until we have been through it. Sometimes in life there are things that we are afraid to do because we don't know how they will turn out. There may be decisions we do not want to make because we are unsure of the consequences. These are closed doors and the one way to find out what is on the other side is to open them.

Take a sheet of paper and imagine you are writing a letter to God. Tell him what the closed doors are in your life – what are the decisions you find hard or the thins you are scared of doing? Write them down and seal them in the envelope so no one else can see them.

God knows which doors are the right ones for you to open. Ask him to give you the wisdom to know which doors to knock on, and the courage to walk through when he opens them.

## SEEK

Jesus said, 'Seek, and you will find' (Matthew 7:7).

Sometimes we do not know where to begin looking for God. Jesus tells us it is important that we do look.

Imagine the map represents your life. Where is God? Is he in the centre, or out on the edge somewhere? Take a red pin and stick it in the map to represent God.

Where are you in relation to God? Are you near him or far away? Take a blue pin and stick it in the map to represent you.

However far away God seems, he is always willing to be found by those who look for him. Think about the distance between the two pins. Would you like this to change? Ask God to help you find him.

## ASK

Jesus said, 'Ask, and God will give to you' (Matthew 7:7).

What do you want to ask God?

Use the magnetic words to ask God your questions.

How do you think God will answer you? Be ready to listen for his answer.

# DECATHLON

## CONSENT FORM

Young person's full name

Address

Emergency contact name

Phone number

GP's name

GP's phone number

Any known allergies or conditions

**I confirm that the above details are complete and correct to the best of my knowledge.**
In the unlikely event of illness or accident, I give permission for any appropriate first aid to be given by the nominated first-aider. In an emergency, and if I cannot be contacted, I am willing for my child to be given hospital treatment, including anaesthetic, if necessary. I understand that every effort will be made to contact me as soon as possible.

SIGNATURE OF PARENT/GUARDIAN

DATE

# DECATHLON

## REGISTRATION FORM

Please use a separate form for each young person

Venue

Dates from

to

Young person's full name

Sex: **M** / **F**

Date of birth

School

Please register my young person for *Decathlon*. Parent's/guardian's signature

Parent's/guardian's full name

Address

Phone number

I give permission for my young person's and my details to be entered on the church database. **Y** / **N**

I give permission for my young person's photograph to be taken during *Decathlon*. **Y** / **N**
(The photographs will be used for church purposes only, including church magazines and press releases.)

# DECATHLON

How has *Decathlon* met the aims that you set out before you started? Use this form to assess what happened, what worked and what you might need to change for the next club that you do.

**1** What were your aims for *Decathlon*? Write them here:

**5** What other successes did you have at *Decathlon*?

**2** How close did you come to meeting each aim? Think about each aim individually and match *Decathlon* as a whole against that aim.

**6** What other problems did you come across?

**3** If you met (or came close to meeting) your aims, what were the factors that contributed to that success?

**7** What will you change for the next event you do? Will your aims be different?

**4** If you didn't meet your aims, what factors contributed to that? Were there influences beyond your control that hindered you?

**8** And finally, how will you continue your work with these young people?

# SAMPLE RISK ASSESSMENT METHOD

## SAMPLE RISK ASSESSMENT METHOD

This is by no means the only way you can risk assess your events, but if you've never done this kind of thing before, this simple five-step method is a good place to start.

## STAGE 1 LOOK FOR THE HAZARDS

A 'hazard' is anything that can cause harm.

These may include lifting heavy equipment, slippery floors, getting lost, blocked fire exits, water, stairs, using ladders, trailing power leads, poor lighting, lit candles.

Start your list with the potential everyday hazards involved in the activity or in using a particular room or area and then work through the risk(s) posed by that hazard. Start with the obvious.

## STAGE 2 WHO IS AT RISK?

A 'risk' is the chance, high or low, that someone may be harmed by the hazard. Which groups of people or individuals might be affected?
Think especially about:
• anyone with disabilities;
• visitors or newcomers;
• inexperienced leaders;
• young children;
• groups meeting at a distance from the main site or building;
• whether any leaders are working alone with groups.

## STAGE 3 HOW WELL IS THE RISK CONTROLLED?

Think through the risks involved. For every hazard, there could be several risks. These may vary in probability and severity – and different people may have different opinions. Don't worry about that – it will be useful to air your ideas and discuss the possibilities: it will all add to your understanding of the safety issues. You may already be taking precautions to reduce the risk, but there is still likely to be some level of risk which may be high, medium or low. Your aim needs to be to make any risk as low as possible.
Consider:
• Are there legal requirements?
• What is good practice?
• Is there expert advice available?
• Can the risk be eliminated?
• Can the risk be controlled, so that harm is unlikely?
• Is there a less risky option?
• Can we do things differently or protect against the hazard?

If the risk is not already adequately controlled, go to Stage 4.

## STAGE 4 RECORD YOUR DECISIONS AND WHAT ACTION IS REQUIRED

This is the critical bit! Think through a number of ways of improving the safety of the situation. You may decide to eliminate the risk by avoiding the hazard completely.

## STAGE 5 REVIEW AND REVISE

Have the measures you've planned or taken reduced the risk? Record the new level of risk here. As a team, decide if your changes are effective – and if not, go through the process again. You may need to follow up this assessment with other people in your church or organisation, maybe a minister, a caretaker or office staff. If you do identify a significant safety issue, don't assume someone else will notice: alert the appropriate person.

# FOLLOWING UP DECATHLON

However you have used the *Decathlon* programme, you will more than likely make contact with young people and families who have little or no regular connection with church. Through *Decathlon*, the young people will have heard truths from the gospel, built positive relationships with your team and enjoyed being in the community. The following ideas aim to enable you to continue the important work you have begun and try to reach and disciple the young people on a more regular basis, turning this *Decathlon* ministry into a year-round ministry to young people who may be currently outside the reach of your church.

## ONGOING GROUPS

You may be able to invite young people to existing groups you have within your church – evening youth groups or Sunday morning groups. Be mindful that welcoming young people from outside your church community into these groups will mean that the groups themselves will need to change to accommodate the new members. You may need to manage this carefully with any group's existing members. Scripture Union, Urban Saints and YFC all produce material for use in groups such as these:

## FROM SCRIPTURE UNION

**theGRID for leaders**
£9.99

**theGRID lifestyle**
£2.99

Out every three months, *theGRID* is packed with ideas to help 11 to 14s engage with the Bible and get to know God better. The leaders' magazine provides all the information to run the session, and the lifestyle magazine provides material for young people to interact with the Bible in more depth.

**SUbstance**
£9.99
Nine volumes

*SUbstance* is a series of nine books, each one containing ten sessions of material to help 14 to 18s meet God and follow him more closely.

**LightLive**
**www.lightlive.org**
Donation-based

Access *theGRID* and *SUbstance* material online, and plunder Scripture Union's archive of material to create exciting and engaging sessions for your youth groups.

## FROM URBAN SAINTS

**Energize**
**www.energize.uk.net/**
Subscription based

The *Energize* website provides a continual stream of adaptable, creative, biblically based meeting plans for 5 to 7s, 7 to 10s, 11 to 14s and 15 to 18s. Your leaders will never run out of ideas! There's also a continual stream of drama sketches, articles and online training tools to inspire, encourage and equip.

## FROM YFC

**Rock Solid, RS2 and Mettle**
**www.resources.yfc.co.uk/**
Subscription based

Reach out to 11 to 14s in your community with *Rock Solid*. Engage with 11 to 14s in your church with RS2. Build courage, spirit and character in 15 to 18s with *Mettle*. These resources are easy to adapt for groups of any size. Whether you are an experienced youth worker or a volunteer just starting out, you will find plenty in these resources to challenge and inspire.

## CREATING A NEW GROUP

You may find that it's best to create a new group for the young people who have been part of *Decathlon*. There are advantages to this, for example, good relationships can be maintained and young people from outside your church community aren't faced with church traditions immediately. You will need to make sure that there are other ways for these young people to start to engage with your community. To help you, you could try:

**Youth Alpha or Christianity Explored**
You may feel that the group of young people you have been working with is ready to try something a bit more challenging. Why not try *Youth Alpha* or *Freedom in Christ* for young people? Go to **www.youthalpha.org** and **www.yfc. co.uk** for more details.

## BIBLE READING

Nearly all young people, regardless of their background, struggle to read the Bible. You may find that challenging young people to a finite programme of Bible reading is the best way to help them start.

**E100Y**
E100Y is a Bible reading programme for young people created by Scripture Union, Bible Society and other partners across the world. It seeks to help young people open up the big story of the Bible through a programme of 100 passages spanning the whole Bible (broken into 20 blocks of five passages). Designed to be done in the community, both online and offline, this resource will really challenge young people and their leaders to read the Bible and meet God. Go to **www. scriptureunion.org.uk** for more details.

## SCHOOLS LINKS

If you have been using *Decathlon* in a school context, you may have developed new relationships with local schools or developed existing ones. How else can you get more involved in schools? You might be able to help with the RE or PSHE/citizenship curriculum. You might also start an after-school club as part of the Extended Schools Initiative. Contact Scripture Union (**www.scriptureunion. org.uk**) or YFC (**www.yfc.co.uk**) for more help on how to do this.